DELTA TEACHER DEVELOPMENT SERIES
Series editors Mike Burghall and Lindsay Clandfield

Spotlight on Learning Styles

Teacher strategies for learner success

Marjorie Rosenberg

Published by
DELTA PUBLISHING
Quince Cottage
Hoe Lane
Peaslake
Surrey GU5 9SW
England

www.deltapublishing.co.uk

© Delta Publishing 2013

ISBN 978-1-905085-71-2

Edited by Mike Burghall
Designed by Christine Cox
Cover photo © David Arts/Shutterstock.com
Printed in Malta by Melita Press

Dedication

This book is dedicated to all those teachers who want to discover what makes their learners special, to those learners who are able to discover something special about themselves and, above all, to my friend, colleague and mentor, April Bowie.

Acknowledgements

This book has been a part of my life for many years, but it could not have come to fruition without the support of Nick Boisseau from DELTA.

I especially want to thank Mike Burghall, whose editing and guidance were truly invaluable in creating a book I can feel proud of. I would also like to thank Christine Cox who visualised what I had written and created the design.

The other people who have inspired me on this journey include:

Brigitte Jug, with whom I have spent many hours discussing the concept of learning styles and their implementation in the classroom. The teacher training seminars we have held together throughout Austria have taught us a great deal about how learners and teachers think – and we have seen the results of our work both in the feedback we get from former participants as well as from students of the teachers who worked with us.

Jim Wingate, who gave a seminar many years ago in Graz and showed me how things could be done differently.

Robert Dilts and Judith DeLosier, whose NLP training in Santa Cruz, California, continues to be a guiding influence in what I do.

Michael Grinder, who brought these techniques to the classroom and introduced me to practical applications.

Finally, my colleagues, students and friends who have tried out the models and checklists, as well as the activities, and have given me feedback on them. I thank all of you collectively – you have all made this possible.

From the author

Every journey begins with the first step, and mine began in Portland, Oregon, in July 1996. I was attending a course by Michael Grinder on new trends in teaching and in a pairwork activity sat next to a young woman from Seattle, Washington, named April Bowie.

We were asked to try out the Swassing-Barbe diagnostic test which determined our preferred input, output and storage channels. While working together, we began talking about our experiences with learning styles – and discovered that we had arrived at this seminar through both similar and dissimilar experiences.

The first time I had heard about the concept of styles was several years earlier in a course in Salzburg on 'superlearning' techniques, based on the idea that we need to make use of both hemispheres of the brain in language learning rather than concentrating on the more analytical left hemisphere.

One afternoon, we were given a task to decide if we were visual, auditory or kinaesthetic learners – and suddenly a world opened up for me. I was finally presented with a concept that helped me to understand that my failure to learn a foreign language in high school may have had to do with the way I was taught rather than my own abilities.

Suddenly, experiences from my time at school began to make sense and I continued on my own to explore various models and ideas connected with styles.

April had taught language arts in a high school in the US and tried to figure out why some of her students learned so much more easily than others. Her curiosity led her to investigate a number of models, and her own research into the area of adolescents and learning styles left her convinced that how people perceived and organised new material played a major role in their success.

We began to collaborate and explore the different possibilities of opening the eyes of both teachers and students to the fact that *how* we learn as individuals is as important as *what* we learn. School systems today are under enormous pressure to demonstrate their achievements, and sometimes this individuality is forgotten along the way.

True innovation and learning take place when the strengths of a learner are built on, and the encouragement given to learners in a 'learning-styles' aware classroom can be exactly what they need to develop and grow. By making use of the three models in this book – Visual, Auditory and Kinaesthetic sensory perception; Global–Analytic cognitive processing; Mind Organisation, based on concrete or abstract perception and systematic or non-systematic organisation of material – April and I put together seminars to spread the word and encourage other teachers to try out these new ideas in their classrooms.

Our teacher training activities took us to the mountains overlooking Innsbruck, to a seminar venue next to the Danube in Vienna, to Edmonton, Canada, and to small towns in the state of Washington, north of Seattle. We both continued looking into ways to help learners find their place in the world of learning, April returning to Auburn, Washington, and me to Graz, Austria, where I still live, teaching students and training teachers.

When April passed away in 2006, continuing in her footsteps became a mission which has continued until today – and the more I learn about the individuals I work with, and the different ways in which each of them learns, the more convinced I am that this was the right path to choose.

My hope with *Spotlight on Learning Styles* is to share the journey with you and to pass on thoughts, ideas and concepts that have been a major part of my life for the last two decades.

Contents

From the author — Page 3

Part A — Page 7

Spotlight on styles — Page 15
Spotlight on success — Page 25

Part B — Page 27

1 Spotlight on strategies — Page 29

Visual, Auditory and Kinaesthetic
learner strategies — Page 30
Global–Analytic learner strategies — Page 32
Mind Organisation learner strategies — Page 34
Teacher strategies — Page 37

**2 Visual, Auditory and Kinaesthetic
learning styles** — Page 39

Visual
What have I changed? — Page 40
What have we changed? — Page 40
What are they wearing? — Page 41
Find the shapes — Page 41
Putting it together — Page 42
I'm looking at something … — Page 42
If I fly to the moon … — Page 43
Whose line is the longest? — Page 43

Auditory
Pass it on! — Page 44
Puzzle it out! — Page 44
Reconstructing cartoons — Page 46
Reconstructing texts — Page 46
What's the joke? — Page 47
Secret identities — Page 48
Let me be your guide — Page 48
Jigsaw listening — Page 49

Kinaesthetic emotional
Emotional objects — Page 49
Positive personalities — Page 50
Horoscope — Page 50
It's in the cards — Page 52
Planning a trip — Page 53
Outlines — Page 53
Roll a mood — Page 54
It makes me feel … — Page 54

Kinaesthetic motoric
It's in the bag — Page 55
Creating a machine — Page 55
Back-writing telephone — Page 56
Mime artist — Page 56
Acting out adverbs — Page 57
Sticky-note body — Page 58
This is my knee — Page 58
Becoming a statue — Page 59

Mixed VAK
Becoming a picture — Page 59
Back-to-back drawing — Page 60
Memory — Page 60
VAK bingo — Page 61
Your last holiday — Page 61
Look: no mistakes! — Page 62
Interesting definitions — Page 62
Who went where? — Page 64
Run and dictate — Page 64
Run and draw — Page 65

Contents

3 **Global–Analytic learning styles**   Page 66

Global

    Write a story   Page 67

    Complete the conditionals   Page 67

    What would you do …?   Page 68

    Circle faces   Page 68

    Listen and change   Page 69

    Buzz words   Page 69

    You–Robot   Page 70

Analytic

    The 'yes-no' hotseat   Page 70

    Do you want to bet?   Page 71

    Mark the map   Page 72

    Detective story   Page 74

    Logic puzzle   Page 74

    What are the rules?   Page 76

    Five in a row   Page 76

    Ask the right question   Page 78

Mixed Global–Analytic

    Initial adjectives   Page 78

    Animal, vegetable, mineral   Page 79

    Coded interviews   Page 80

    Roll an answer   Page 80

    Word hunt   Page 81

    It's on the box   Page 82

    The envelope game   Page 82

4 **Mind Organisation learning styles**   Page 83

Flexible Friend

    Personal goals   Page 84

    Emotional dictation   Page 85

    Deep impact   Page 86

    All about my partner   Page 86

    Personal mindmaps   Page 87

    What we have in common   Page 87

Expert Investigator

    The perfect page   Page 88

    Just give me the facts   Page 88

    Nothing but the facts   Page 90

    Internet investigation   Page 90

    Researching an excursion   Page 91

Power Planner

    How does it work?   Page 91

    Is everything in order?   Page 92

    Group grammar   Page 92

    Confirming information   Page 93

    Setting priorities   Page 93

    Linking ideas   Page 94

Radical Reformer

    Radical roleplay   Page 95

    Act out the characters   Page 96

    Can you sell it?   Page 97

    The restaurant game   Page 97

    When I was a child …   Page 98

    Our ideal home   Page 98

Mixed Mind Organisation

    The department store   Page 99

    Our type of trip   Page 99

    Don't say the word!   Page 100

    My first time …   Page 101

    Your last chance   Page 102

Part C   Page 103

    Further approaches   Page 105

    Further activities   Page 109

    Further reading   Page 114

    From spotlight to springboard   Page 116

From the editors   Page 117

From the publisher   Page 118

'I never knew there were different styles of learning. I thought I just couldn't ever learn a foreign language.'

A visual learner, after trying to learn French through the audio-lingual method

Spotlight on learning styles

Teachers are increasingly confronted not only with mixed-ability *classes* but also the diverse needs of their individual *learners*. Spotlighting different learning styles, especially when accompanied by ideas and activities and differentiated according to learner preference, can be a very supportive tool.

Teachers are generally aware they have to teach to different learner types as well as establish rapport with them, but they have neither the background nor the time to search for appropriate material. Once they see how easy it can be to slightly adapt activities for different learners, they become more interested in discovering new possibililities for their classrooms.

This book is in no way an attempt to pigeon-hole learners or to narrow teaching opportunities. Rather, it is intended as a tool to stretch both learners and teachers and to encourage them to try out methods outside their usual 'comfort zones'. In addition, a major aim is to create tolerance for those whose learning styles are different from our own.

Learning styles

When we talk of learning styles, what exactly are we talking about? The styles which will be addressed, and around which *Spotlight on Learning Styles* is organised, are:

1 VAK. Visual, auditory and kinaesthetic sensory channels are often referred to as the perceptual filters used to analyse how learners first take in, store and recall information. Basic research in this area was carried out by Walter Barbe and Raymond Swassing [1] in the 1970s with their investigation and testing of what they called 'modality preferences'.

2 Global and **Analytic**. The second model of learner types deals with cognitive processing. This is based on research carried out by Herman Witkin from the late 1940s until the 1970s [2]. Witkin developed a test called the 'Group Embedded Figures Test' which determines how globally or analytically a person cognitively processes information.

3 Mind Organisation. This model of perception and organisation was based on several different models, and further developed by April Bowie in the mid 1990s [3]. Bowie dealt with both adolescent and adult learners, setting up a system to establish how people first take in information (either concretely or abstractly) and then how they process it (either systematically or non-systematically).

Teaching styles

It is important that teachers first begin to recognise characteristics of their own teaching styles. They will need to discover their own profile and be shown how to implement different ideas in their individual teaching situations.

Learners and their learning styles

If you read through evaluations completed by learners after a language course, you may be struck by the fact that learner expectations, as well as preferences, can differ widely. A single group of seemingly harmonious (and in some cases even somewhat homogeneous) learners tends to view and assess classroom activities in completely different ways:

- Some feel that they learned best through language games, speaking activities and discussions about themselves using classwork and groupwork. These students may comment that they feel they needed more student-talking time to practise the language.
- Others feel that they learned best when they had time to reflect and work alone at their own pace. They may say that they feel they had to work in groups too often and were not corrected enough by the teacher or were not given enough language drills to practise with.

The reason for these two widely different impressions of the same group can be partially traced back to the individual learning styles of the course participants. Even in a group where the goals were reached, some learners may feel that they would have liked more – or less – of particular activities and tasks.

It is generally accepted among educators today that learners learn in different ways. As Jeremy Harmer [4] says:

'The moment we realise that a class is composed of individuals (rather than being some kind of unified whole), we have to start thinking about how to respond to those students individually so that while we may frequently teach the group as a whole, we will also, in different ways, pay attention to the different identities we are faced with.'

Pat Burke Guild and Stephen Garger [5] continue in this vein to point out that *'it is possible to strive for uniform outcomes but to intentionally diversify the means for achieving them'.*

Most of us can remember classes where, as learners ourselves, we felt lost – due to the teaching style of a particular instructor. The lucky ones among us either learned to 'translate' the material into the style we were most comfortable using, or we found another person who was able to explain the material in a way which better suited our comprehension abilities. Reasons for this disparity between teaching and learning often have to do with the dichotomy between the learning styles of teacher and learner.

Preference and perception

Research by Anton Gregorc (1982) [6], Rita and Kenneth Dunn (1975) [7] and Walter Barbe and Raymond Swassing (1979) [8], among others, has determined that individuals have their preferred modes of dealing with the intake and processing of information, as well as storage and recall. If learners need different input from what is being provided by their teacher, they may not be able to cope with the material. According to several researchers, including the founders of Neuro-Linguistic Programming Richard Bandler and John Grinder (1979) [9], we all have filters in place which sort out the enormous amount of information bombarding us from every direction. These filters represent our preferred style of perception.

Our strengths and weaknesses are often set early on and if, by using them, we are successful, we continue to do so. If we are *not* successful in our styles, we find a way to adapt – or simply stop learning a particular subject. Michael Grinder explores these strengths and weaknesses in *Righting the Educational Conveyor Belt* (1991) [10], where he points out the effect that modalities (defined by Barbe and Swassing as *'any of the sensory channels through which an individual receives and retains information'* [11]) have on our learning. He does stress, however, that in the average classroom most learners can move between modalities in order to take in the necessary information. There are also learners who perceive *input* in one modality and easily store or recall information for *output* in another.

But for those learners who are unable to do this easily – and are therefore forced to 'translate' between modalities – it is often up to us, their teachers, to find ways to reach them and facilitate their learning.

'I really loved learning with the language lab. I found that I remembered what I heard and later I bought cassettes that went along with the books. This is the most comfortable way for me to absorb information – much better than reading about it in a book.'

An adult auditory learner

'I was really happy to discover through a diagnostic test that I was very kinaesthetic and worked best when I could touch things. I was finally able to convince my parents to let me train as a chef rather than continue in an abstract academic field where I felt uncomfortable.'

A kinaesthetic motoric learner

Learners and their teachers

We tend to teach our learners in the way that we were able to learn best ourselves. As we are comfortable doing this, we do not always take the time to adjust our teaching to meet learners' myriad needs. Some background information on learning styles and their application in the classroom can be a valuable tool for teachers looking for new ways to expand their repertoire and reach a larger number of their learners.

Observing groups of learners work on a task can be fascinating. I once watched a class work on a jigsaw puzzle set up as a language activity. The pieces were cut as normal jigsaw puzzle pieces and had sentences written on them. However, as the groups were only told to put the puzzle together but not *how* to do it, they approached the task very differently.

- One group put the pieces together first and completely ignored the language.
- The other group read the language aloud and then decided which piece came next.

Two totally different approaches to the same problem!

- Other learners, when given the choice, will immediately turn to a partner or find a group to work in to complete a task.
- Others much prefer to tackle a task on their own.

Differences and difficulties

'I never realised that I used so much visual language (I see. Is it clear? Just picture this.) until I asked a colleague to observe my class. Now I try to use other words to reach different learner styles.'

A teacher

The question then remains: How do we incorporate these differences in our lesson plans and course design? Learners need to be *engaged* in order to learn a language. They make choices between different learning techniques. Today's classrooms frequently provide them with visual aids in the form of PowerPoint presentations, OHTs, posters, mind-maps, DVD players and audio aids such as CD players and podcasts.

There are also specific strategies used in common by most successful language learners – these include guessing, taking risks with new language, trying out new forms, and developing an awareness of words which fit together and structures which have implied meaning.

Inclusive teaching today includes finding ways to reach different types of learners. As it is impossible to teach simultaneously to all styles at the same time, teachers have to learn to adapt their styles somewhat in order to convey information. 'Diversity' is a word often used in discussions about up-to-date teaching methods, although most schools still strive for uniformity. 'Teaching to the test' is only one example of this trend, while 'teaching to the learner' would be a better motto. [12]

It is clear that working with large groups of learners is difficult enough without taking individual preferences into account, but there needs to be a balance between efficiency (teaching as much material as possible) and the real imparting of information (teaching to learners of different styles in a way which is comprehensible to them). This calls for raised consciousness on the part of the educator – and *making use* of this knowledge to decide what to do. Once we are aware of the styles present in our classroom, we can decide when to 'harmonise' with them (teach in the way our learners learn best) or when to 'challenge' them (teach in a way in which the learners find it necessary to reach out of their preferred style). [13]

Definitions and development

'Style' can be defined as patterns of behavior and the approaches we use regularly with the aim of reaching particular goals. Expanding on this idea, we can look at how the researchers in the field define styles:

- Keefe (1979) says that styles are *'characteristic cognitive, affective and psychological behaviours that serve as relatively stable indicators of how learners perceive, interact with, and respond to the learning environment'*. [14]
- Reid (1995) explains style as *'internally based characteristics, often not perceived or used consciously, that are the basis for the intake of new information'*. [15]
- Kinsella (1995) says that *'learning style refers to an individual's natural, habitual and*

preferred ways of absorbing, processing and retaining new information and skills which persist regardless of teaching methods of content area'. She concludes that *'everyone has a learning style, but each person's is as unique as a signature'.* [16]

- Cohen (2002) states: *'Indeed we learn in different ways and what suits one learner may be inadequate for another. While learning styles seem to be relatively stable, teachers can modify the learning tasks they use in their classes in a way that may bring the best out of particular learners with particular learning style preferences. It is also possible that learners over time can be encouraged to engage in 'style-stretching' so as to incorporate approaches to learning they were resisting in the past.'* [17]

In practical application of the information above, Dunn and Dunn [18] say that optimal conditions for language learning occur when the preferred style matches the learning environment, the methods and the resources offered. The development of styles is a continual process: they are created early on (whether by nature or nurture has not been determined) but go through stages of modification. Generally, if the strategies which emerge prove to be successful they will be enforced – change generally comes when a person sees that they have to modify their strategies in order to achieve a goal.

Limits and limitations

It is important to keep in mind that determining learning styles should not be seen in any way as a limitation on what a person can or cannot do. The limits that define our worlds can be extended and broadened: knowing our style may be the springboard to doing just that. In addition, there are some other factors to bear in mind. The profile that results from doing style checklists may also depend on other factors:

- One is temporal: you may get a different picture at the beginning, middle or end of your career or learning journey. We often take on different roles as we move through life, and this can affect the outcome of a questionnaire designed to test a learning style. In addition, many of us learn to adapt and change along the way – so that we may answer questions differently at different periods of our lives.
- Another is situational: if you think of specific places or situations when answering the questions, the answers may vary if the situations are different. Other skills may come into play, of course, depending on the task at hand – and this can certainly have an influence on how we interpret a question, and the answer we give to it.

This is not to say that learning styles are the *only* factor which determines whether or not learning takes place, but they can certainly contribute to it. Sometimes, just adding a short activity to a lesson can broaden the appeal to different learner styles and be an efficient way of increasing the knowledge and motivation of a learner.

The activities in *Spotlight on Learning Styles* are designed to help teachers reach uniform goals, while taking different paths to get to them. They can be used with any coursebook or tailored material.

Teachers and their learners

It is doubtful that any of us will have a class of learners who are homogeneous as far as their learning styles are concerned – whatever activity we do will most likely appeal more to one learner type than another, but some will also help learners to stretch out of their styles. And by incorporating a *mix* of methods, we can reach more learners than if we always teach using the same ones. Simply understanding that learners are different is already a first step. The idea behind this book is to show teachers how easily they can make use of the variety of types in their classrooms.

Awareness

Most teachers strive to include all learners in their lessons but, sometimes, they simply do not know how to adapt their teaching styles to a learner whose style is very different from

'I was really frustrated in a class until I discovered that I needed to see and touch things but the teacher preferred talking to us and using CDs. But once I knew what I needed, I could practise at home – which helped my self-confidence and then I began to enjoy the class more.'

A visual and kinaesthetic motoric adult learner

'I never understood why some learners felt they needed to have all the background information about a topic until I realised that it was just their style. I had thought that they were just trying to be annoying.'

A teacher

their own. Knowledge of how learners perceive, process and store information can help them to become more flexible – and more efficient at conveying information to their learners. In addition, when teachers recognise their *own* styles, they become aware of what they have been doing to convey information and which style has been most comfortable for them. In teacher training seminars, in-service teachers are often surprised at how simple it can be to slightly adapt an activity to cater to their learners' needs.

- One teacher trainer was shocked at feedback from a group who criticised him for not giving out the written materials at the beginning of the teacher training course. As he learns best by listening, he thought that the handouts he had prepared would distract the participants so he held them back till the end – this action had the opposite effect, however, as a number of the teachers in the course simply felt lost without the written word as their styles differed from that of the trainer and they wanted to 'see' what he was talking about.
- A teacher expressed surprised when learners complained that a course contained too many activities and didn't provide enough grammar rules and structure. The teacher most probably chose the best activities for conveying the information – and simply had not considered the fact that the learners had different needs.
- Another teacher did not understand why her learners commented on their evaluation forms that they would have liked more speaking practice during the class. This teacher felt that she had balanced the activities well – but also worried at times that she was not 'teaching' enough.

Most teachers would agree that learners are generally open to materials which help them to learn and which they enjoy doing. When an activity is geared towards a particular learner type, that learner feels more 'at home' – thereby adding to the success of a lesson. Therefore, by understanding how learners process and remember information, we can take the first steps towards learner-centred classrooms.

Supplementary material can also have the advantage of reinforcing the learning effect and helping the learner to have a different approach to material. Using a variety of materials is one way to optimise learner success, something all teachers and learners certainly aim for. When learners *enjoy* learning, their self-esteem and motivation increase, creating a cycle of positive experiences. In addition, learners can be encouraged to become aware of their own learning style strengths, thus giving them tools they can use to learn on their own.

Autonomy

The advantage of supplementary and flexible materials is that they can be integrated into normal lessons to allow for the risk-taking and practice necessary for language acquisition. When we encourage them look at their own learning from a meta-cognitive position, our learners can discover for themselves how different activities will enlarge their repertoire of skills – this is also a way to lead them down the path to becoming more autonomous learners.

Learners who are given the assessment tools found in Chapter One of this book – 'Spotlight on strategies' have reported very positive reactions to them. They found that they were able to become aware of *how* they learned and not only *how well* or *what* they learned. Learner journals have been used successfully by Thomas Roche [19] to explore the manner by which learners approach tasks:

- Teachers who contribute by adopting curricula to suit learners' styles can improve outcomes.
- Learners who are encouraged to examine their individual preferences can also adopt successful strategies on their own.

According to Roche, change is not random [20]. Learners who are encouraged through the design of lessons can stretch out of their 'comfortable' styles to take on successful strategies, and these effective strategies can be used by a wide range of learners. This is where the

'It was interesting to watch a group working away at an activity until I reminded them that the class had ended ten minutes ago. When I commented that they had said they didn't like 'games', they answered that this activity was different because it needed logical thinking to do.'

A teacher in an evening class

flexibility of the teacher also comes into play. How learners perceive information has an effect on the strategies they are willing to adopt when they approach a task but, if the result is successful use of language, teachers may have to learn to accept these different approaches as perfectly natural.

As Harmer says: '*We want to satisfy the many different students in front of us, teaching to their individual strengths with activities designed to produce the best results for each of them, yet we also want to address our teaching to the group as a whole.*' [21] He goes on to comment that '*our task as teachers will be greatly helped if we can establish* **who** *the different students in our classes are and recognise* **how** *they are different*'. (The emphasis is mine.)

Once we have some idea of how our learners are different, we can also be of help when they approach us to ask how they can best learn when they are away from the classroom. Many learners have fixed ideas about what is right and wrong when it comes to learning. Telling a visual learner to listen to CDs or an auditory learner to 'picture words' may lead to more frustration.

Often when learners receive suggestions that match their styles, they are happy to implement them – and often come back with positive feedback and more ideas of their own. Once they have a good idea of their strengths, they often find ways themselves to expand their approaches to learning and develop a set of strategies and techniques which work for them.

Teachers and their teaching styles

As teachers, however, it is absolutely essential that we understand that it is not possible to put learners into neat little boxes by using assessment tools such as those provided in 'Spotlight on strategies' (or through our own observation of learners). Just when we think that we are sure that we know how someone will approach a task, that person may surprise us by doing exactly the opposite. What they do may also depend on the particular material, how the learner perceives the information or the group dynamics in a particular class – this also has an effect on the strategies used and the level of involvement and motivation of the learners.

An important point to make here is that individual styles are not an excuse. Learners sometimes feel relieved when they discover that their learning difficulties stem from having a different style to their teacher. Respect for different styles is one thing, using a style preference to 'get out of' doing a task is another – and certainly not the point of this book. It should be looked at as a two-way street:

- It is the responsibility of the *learner* to discover means of adapting to different modes of instruction.
- It is the responsibility of the *teacher* to help the learner to learn to do that. [22]

It is important to reiterate, however, that many teachers tend to teach in the way they themselves learn best. This means that their individual learning styles will generally be reflected in their teaching. As the teacher may be better-equipped to adapt to different styles, it is also important for them to become aware of how they teach and to look at these methods from a learning style point of view. This is the first step to discovering how to emerge from our personal 'comfort zone' in order to reach learners who have *other* strengths and weaknesses.

The three models described at the beginning of these pages will be dealt with in detail in 'Spotlight on styles', where the characteristics of each of the models are explained and discussed and information is included about both learners' and teachers' styles in order to clarify more exactly how, as teachers, we may be 'matching' or 'mismatching' a particular style or learner.

There may be some questions as to why Neuro-Linguistic Programming (NLP) and Multiple Intelligences (MI) are not explicitly dealt with at this point. Processing information through

'*I had a learner who got on everyone's nerves but mine. I found him so fascinating to observe, as I always wondered what he would do next. Knowing about style made my life in the classroom much more pleasant.*'

A teacher

'*I was never good at spelling out loud. I always needed to write a word down and look at it to make sure it was correct.*'

A 60-year-old teacher who is primarily visual

the VAK sensory channels was known by educators long before it became an element of NLP, but the reason for not focusing on NLP extensively here is that it is not a learning style in itself. Similarly, Multiple Intelligences are perceived by the author as 'talents' and 'abilities' – rather than learning styles *per se*. Both these approaches, however, are discussed in Part C, and teachers are invited to follow up their interest in the 'Further reading' section on page 114.

Spotlight on learning

Misconceptions

Styles are neither 'right' or 'wrong' – they are 'valueless'. No one style is better than another style – it just may be that one style is more conducive for learning a particular type of material, or in a particular type of school. Each style has its strong and weak points. In addition, learners need to learn to step out of their personal comfort zones in order to optimise their learning capabilities. [23]

It is also necessary not to confuse *style* and *competence*. There are times when we do stop learning a particular subject because of the teaching methods or the fact that we don't enjoy it, but if something is important enough to us we learn to adapt our styles in order to achieve a goal. Getting a driver's licence in some countries involves learning about the engine of the car, a daunting task for those of us who do not feel particularly technically gifted. However, if we want to drive we have to learn the material somehow, or be content with using public transport, cycling – or walking!

This holds true for learners as well. A learner who had taken part in a learning strategies course told his teacher: *'I now realise that I am not slow, I am global / kinaesthetic.'* As most school systems are set up to teach to a specific type of learner, learners outside the general scope may become frustrated and feel that they do not belong. Once they discover that there are no 'good or bad' styles and that styles themselves do not indicate mental capacities for learning, they can begin to cultivate their own strengths and build on them. This gives these learners the opportunity to develop individually and make decisions as to how and what they feel they should be learning.

Learners may actually discover that there is a 'mismatch' with the school system or study programme they are currently enrolled in and make a change to a subject or school which fits them better.

- Learners obviously have to first *discover* their style and then *try out* different methods and strategies to optimise their own learning progress.
- Teachers have the opportunity to help learners on their quest for knowledge by encouraging them to discover for themselves what they need and how to ask for it.

Whether this discovery involves a major or a minor change will depend on many factors, and the ultimate decision must be up to the learner. However, making the information available is how teaching and learning becomes a two-way street.

Motivation

Success is often cited as a motivating factor. After all, when we see our own progress or find that we truly enjoyed a lesson, positive feelings lead to an increase in motivation. In addition, learners who feel that a teacher is interested in them and truly understands their needs, goals and wishes are generally more encouraged to try hard. Praise can be a powerful motivator in and outside the classroom.

Motivation can also stem from the ability on the part of the teacher to establish and maintain rapport with the learners.

- Learners who feel that we understand their individual needs gain the confidence that they can learn from us.
- Learners sense intuitively if we care about them as individuals and accept them as people.

Listening to our learners and taking their suggestions on board (when possible) makes them more comfortable in our classroom and gives them the feeling that we also have an interest in seeing them do well. In *In Your Hands – NLP in ELT*, Jane Revell and Susan Norman stated: '*Rapport is maximising similarities and minimising differences between people at a non-conscious level.*' [24] When we achieve this, certain barriers to learning can be overcome, creating a successful dialogue between teacher and learner.

It is up to us, as educators, to acknowledge that learners possess stronger and weaker talents and abilities that we are ready to work with in order to set up a relationship which is positive and useful for learning. In situations where we are able to create this feeling in the classroom, learners feel respected and their motivational level is raised. Motivated learners with self-confidence are more likely to try out language and develop good learner strategies (Dörnyei 2001) [25].

When rapport is present, a classroom climate is created which is conducive to experiment, trial and error, and taking chances. The supportive and positive classroom can be called a 'safe zone' [26] where learners feel confident enough to risk making mistakes in order to develop beyond basic language, and are helped in finding and developing their ideal and individual learning methods, leading to increased motivation for both learners and teachers.

Spotlight on teaching

Implications

Teachers may ask themselves why it is so important to explore the different styles in our classrooms. As many of us have large groups of mixed-ability learners, this may seem like another enormous task we need to undertake. However, once we begin to notice how our learners are best able to learn, the cycle of learning becomes more enjoyable and leads to real progress. By encouraging learners to develop those strategies which will make them more autonomous in how they approach and work on material, we can help them to become life-long learners.

Learning styles can usually be observed at an early age. However, they may change over time – as people learn to adapt to their environments. The goal here is not to pigeon-hole learners or teachers, but to offer both self-knowledge and awareness, and to create a feeling of tolerance for others.

> '*Thank you so much for taking away my fear. For the first time, I am not afraid to talk even if the others in the class are better than I am.*'
>
> An email from an adult learner

The strategies included in this book are general ideas, and teachers need to feel comfortable using them as well. But once we have experienced the joy of a learner who begins to feel they are truly learning, our enthusiasm for what we are doing builds. According to Dörnyei: '*Such a commitment towards the subject matter then becomes 'infectious', instilling in students a similar willingness to pursue knowledge.*' [27]

- Teachers become more motivating (and motivated) teachers.
- Learners become more motivated learners, a 'state-of-being' which has all the elements of success.

Implementation

The practical implementation of using learning styles in the classroom remains an individual choice on the part of the teacher.

One way to begin is to give our learners checklists, inviting them to fill them out and discuss them in class. This is definitely a way to make them aware of how they approach learning.

Another possibility is simply to expand on our own style of teaching:

- We can record ourselves and make notes of the words and methods we use to see if we concentrate on one particular style.
- We can ask another person to observe us.
- We can even ask our learners to comment on the activities or teaching methods they are comfortable or uncomfortable with.

This has to be up to the teacher, as every institution, class and teaching situation is different. However, becoming aware that there will most likely be a wide range of learning styles among the individuals sitting in front of us may be the first step to looking into stretching out of the way we usually approach teaching.

We may notice that we need to write more often on the board or give out handouts at the beginning of a class or organise our materials differently in order to satisfy the needs of different learners.

This also allows us to establish rapport more easily, as having a 'tool box' of different methods and activities gives us the flexibilty to respond to a broader group of learners and their needs.

Classroom management plays a role here as well, and it may be necessary to give up certain pre-suppositions and change the way we deal with problems in the classroom:

- If a learner constantly asks what a word means in L1, it is possible to make that learner responsible for looking it up in the dictionary and telling the others or writing it down. That gives the responsibility back to the learner, but also satisfies the real need of the individual.
- If a learner finds errors in something we have prepared, that person can become an 'official' proof-reader, giving them status but also giving us a second pair of eyes to look at the materials we produce.
- If a learner is discovered to be extremely kinaesthetic, we may ask them to help out when we demonstrate words by miming and taking part in roleplays or by helping another learner and lending them emotional support.

In sum, the more we know about those we are charged with 'teaching', the better our chances to create a cycle of knowledge which can then flow in both directions – enriching all involved.

Before we proceed to the activities in Part B, we can get to know more about the styles themselves and how to approach them in a practical manner:

Spotlight on styles

Visual, Auditory and Kinaesthetic	Global–Analytic	Mind Organisation

As each person is different, the combination of the three styles leads to a more complete picture of the strengths of each individual person. This information can help both learners and teachers to understand what they need to be more successful and can create their optimal learning or teaching situations. In other words:

Spotlight on success

Spotlight on Learning Styles aims to make both teaching and learning a positive and successful experience – by focusing on the 'how' of acquiring knowledge rather than the 'what' we acquire.

Visual, Auditory and Kinaesthetic

'Modalities' are familiar to most teachers, and many are aware of the importance of multi-sensory teaching and learning although they don't always spot individual learners' styles in their classrooms. Most learners have learned to adapt, meaning that the characteristics that determine one style may not be immediately apparent. We all have the capability of perceiving, processing, storing and remembering information in a visual, auditory or kinaesthetic manner.

We are constantly bombarded with information and, in order to keep from being overwhelmed, we set up a series of filters which include these perceptual channels. However:

- In a relaxed state, we generally have access to all of our systems.
- In stressful situations, we tend to use a primary and (sometimes) a secondary system in which we perceive, process and store information. [28]

This is when the problems associated with not understanding material may arise. Michael Grinder points out that using only one channel can also have an effect on how successful we are in school or other learning situations – depending on whether or not we are then able to access the stored information. In his landmark work *Righting the Educational Conveyor Belt* [29] he goes on to define characteristics of learners, concentrating on their perceptual and sensory channels, as well as pinpointing these styles in teaching methods and concentrating on the classic visual, auditory and kinaesthetic learners.

However, in my own work with adult learners it became clear that the kinaesthestic channel encompassed different characteristics and behaviours – for those who were primarily motoric or tactile, and those who were emotional. This style has therefore been divided into two sections for this book.

Spotlight on visual learners

Visual learners need to see everything written down. They often write out words to check the spelling. They mark their materials with different colours or highlighters, and often organise them with dividers. These learners take notes in class and generally have good handwriting. It is important for them to get handouts from a teacher. They like to have visual stimulation around them, either in the classroom or at home. However, because they remember where they saw something on a page, they need to take the material 'off' the page, rewrite it, rearrange it and learn it again.

When visual learners try to access information they have learned, they generally look up, as that is where they have it stored. When their eyes come back to a level position, they are ready to communicate with another person. [30]

Spotlight on auditory learners

Auditory learners need to listen or to speak in order to remember information. They often sub-vocalise when reading, or turn away from a speaker in order to concentrate on what they hear. They may move in rhythm as if they were listening to an inner beat (teachers interpret this as 'K' but – in rhythm – it is 'A') or make rhythmical noises while learning, and sometimes find that they concentrate best when listening to music in the background, as they often do not enjoy being surrounded by silence. They love class discussions and enjoy telling and listening to stories. They can repeat back what they have heard and their pronunciation is generally quite good.

Some of these learners need to think aloud, and they appreciate someone taking the time to explain something to them carefully. They are not big note-takers, as taking notes may distract them from careful listening, and their handwriting is normally not as consistent and legible as that of visual learners.

'I found it almost impossible to learn a language only by speaking and not seeing the words written out.'

A visual learner

'If only someone would read me the material I have to learn.'

A 22-year-old business student who had been observed as being auditory from the age of four

Auditory learners learn sequentially (from the beginning to the end, much in the way most of us learned the alphabet), which means that they often need to go back to the beginning of a story and 'listen' to it all again – so they may be slower when it comes to finding an answer. When they prepare for written tests, they need to write the material down in order to give themselves a second storage channel, for example the visual one.

Auditory learners tend to look to the side (in the direction of their ears) when they are trying to remember something. As with the other learners, they are ready to speak when their eyes move back and they look straight ahead. [31]

Spotlight on kinaesthetic learners

Kinaesthetic learners combine both *feelings* and *movement* into their learning preferences. Through observation, it appears that these are often closely tied together in children, whereas young adults begin to show a split in these two kinaesthetic models.

Many adults clearly show preferences between 'kinaesthetic emotional' preferences and 'kinaesthetic motoric' ones.

- **Kinaesthetic emotional learners** need to feel comfortable in a group. They can have problems learning if they think the other learners or the teacher don't like them. They also need to connect learning and the material to be learned with positive experiences. If they have failed once at a task or had a negative experience doing something, they may not be willing to try it again.
  They also need to personalise their learning materials. If they are in a regimented system in which this is frowned upon, they may demonstrate more learning difficulties than if they are allowed the freedom to be creative with their own learning. It can be helpful for them to learn how to put their feelings aside and concentrate on the material. In some cases, they have to find their own reasons for learning, and this can overcome some of the negative feelings they may have.
- **Kinaesthetic motoric learners**, on the other hand, need to try everything out for themselves. They learn by doing and through real-life experiences. Moving about is enjoyable for them, but they also learn with flashcards and other manipulatives. They often have trouble sitting for a long period of time, and need more frequent breaks than other learner types. Sometimes they get up during a lesson – just to move about.
  They tend to remember the whole experience rather than the details. When they learn at home, it is necessary for them to also write the material down, as they tend to learn while walking about. During an exam, they may even remember what they were doing when they learned a particular item, and this can help them to recall it.

Both types of kinaesthetic learner tend to look down when they are trying to access experiences or emotions. They look up again when they are ready to express their thoughts. [32]

Spotlight on visual teachers

Visual teachers are, according to Michael Grinder, those who rely on visual aids to get their ideas across. They learn and teach through seeing and observation, and like to have visually stimulating environments. They generally make sure that they have access to a board or presentation slides with written or illustrated materials which can be presented to learners. These teachers also take time to make handouts look special and may add illustrations or cartoons and spend time on formatting. If they have their own classrooms, they generally enjoy decorating the walls with posters or other visually attractive material.

They tend to use language incorporating visual words such as in '*Do you see what I mean?*' or '*Is that clear?*' They may use mind-maps to explain the points they would like to get across, and they like to make use of colour-coded systems, both for the organisation of material as well as while teaching concepts. In addition, they speak somewhat faster than auditory and kinesthetic teachers do and their voices may be somewhat higher pitched.

'I know I failed that test – the teacher didn't smile when she handed it out so I had a terrible feeling and couldn't concentrate very well.'
A kinaesthetic emotional learner

'If I don't try something out myself, I can never do it. Just watching another person is simply not enough.'
A 50-year-old engineer who is primarily kinaesthetic motoric

'I really like learners to turn in homework which has been neatly typed and laid out.'
A visual teacher

Spotlight on auditory teachers

Auditory teachers learn and teach by listening and talking. They therefore rely more on their voices and external audio materials to convey information. They often bring music into the classroom and tend to use a lot of discussion techniques with learners. Their own collection of CDs or other auditory material may be quite comprehensive and they frequently look for ways to integrate this material into their teaching. They are also the teachers who generally work more vigorously on pronunciation or language drills.

Auditory teachers enjoy telling stories and find ways to incorporate storytelling into their classes. They use fewer visual aids than visual teachers, and tend to acknowledge input from learners by repeating it or paraphrasing it. They also speak more slowly and rhythmically than visual teachers.

Spotlight on kinaesthetic emotional teachers

Kinaesthetic emotional teachers learn and teach by using feelings and intuition. They like to use activities in which learners become involved on a more personal and emotional level, and may talk about themselves and their feelings. They often look for activities which bring a personal touch into the classroom while remaining sensitive to the feelings of the learners. They want to feel that learners are truly involved in the activities and the subject matter.

They may also use their own personal stories in order to teach concepts, and tend to know more about their learners' lives outside the classroom. They speak somewhat slower than the other types, but make use of emotions when they express themselves. It is important to these teachers that the learners like them and that there is a harmonious atmosphere in the class.

Spotlight on kinaesthetic motoric teachers

Kinaesthetic motoric teachers learn and teach through the use of movement and physical activities. These teachers demonstrate a great deal of energy in the classroom and rarely sit or stand in one place while teaching. As they look for ways to use physical activities to get concepts across, they often like to make use of mime or other activities, such as roleplays and simulations, which get the learners moving. They may also bring in manipulatives, in order to let the learners touch and move items around.

They may evaluate learners by observing what they do and how they interact with each other. They prefer to explain concepts through demonstrations, and may put less emphasis on using grammar rules while focusing on more functional language. If they have their own classrooms, they may try to set up a comfortable corner where learners can relax. They generally speak the slowest and have the lowest-pitched voices.

Although most of us tend to have our strengths in one or two of the modalities, mixed-modality learning gives us a better chance of success. Put very simply, we can use the metaphor of our brains being similar to a large filing cabinet in which we store experiences or knowledge according to our individual preferences. When we have a fact stored in more than one place it makes it easier to find when we need it, especially if we are stressed or under time pressure. By offering learners materials in more than one way, we can help them to improve their access to what they have learned.

- As *teachers*, it is not difficult to learn to find a way to help all our learners to understand new concepts. This can be as simple as learning how to change the language we use to explain things. By saying *'Let me show you'*, *'I'll tell you how it works'*, *'I'll try to give you a feeling for it'* or *'I can walk you through it step-by-step'*, we are beginning to reach learners in their own 'worlds'. This may take some getting used to – it is, however, definitely worth it in the long run, as the chance of reaching more people in a group is certainly higher.
- As *learners*, discovering ideas which help them to learn and are comfortable to use, they are often rewarded by experiencing a new outlook on learning.

Global–Analytic

Many of us first became acquainted with learning styles through the early definitions of 'right-brained' and 'left-brained' learners. This was based on discoveries in the 1960s made by a team of researchers led by Dr Roger Sperry who physically separated the two hemispheres of the brain by cutting through the 'corpus callosum' of a patient with epilepsy. It soon became clear that certain tasks could only be done by using one side of the brain or the other. These experiments were carried out by applying stimuli to different sides of the body. In general, the researchers found out that the left hemisphere specialised in verbal communication and language, and the right in visual and construction tasks [33]. Sperry went on to win the Nobel Prize in Medicine in 1981 for his work in this field.

The ramifications of these experiments had a great influence on teaching. The basic idea behind these theories was:

- The left hemisphere of the brain, which was responsible for language, also contained the short-term memory.
- The right hemisphere, which was responsible for images, creativity and music, contained the long-term memory.

The main emphasis was then on methods which combined the two halves of the brain – allowing language (or other learned knowledge) to be retained in long-term memory.

As research continued to advance, discoveries were made showing that the right and left split was not as clear-cut as had once been thought. Through the more advanced possibilities for gathering images of the brain available to researchers today, they have discovered that there is more connection between the two halves. How we store and access material also depends on education, background or experience. For example, music had traditionally been thought of as a 'right brain' activity. By using Positron Emission Tomography (PET) scans or other advanced imaging techniques such as Magnetic Resonance Imaging (MRI), scientists could observe the level of activity in different parts of the brain and determine, for example, that trained musicians actually processed music on the left side of the brain, as they tended to analyse it more than non-musicians. [34]

Herman Witkin began his studies of cognitive processing in the 1940s and continued working in the field until the late 1970s. His first discoveries came when working with pilots – that some were more influenced by their surroundings than others – and he developed his theories of field-dependence and field-independence. Analytic, or field-independent, learners tend to be less affected by their environment and more able to concentrate totally on the task in hand, whereas the global, or field-dependent, learners are always aware of what is going on around them and listen more to what their bodies are telling them.

This was first tested by Witkin [35] in 1977 through the Group-Embedded Figures Test (GEFT) which had learners find geometric figures hidden in other geometric figures within a certain period of time. Witkin and others felt that the more figures one finds, the more field-independent or 'analytic' the person is, as finding the figures means ignoring the distractions of the other figures. By the same token, those who are distracted by the other figures are more field-dependent or 'global'.

The test is still used today, and is considered one of the most accurate for determining style. However, learners who are more global find fewer items and may feel at a disadvantage – which is one reason for using different testing methods in addition to this test. Today, educators tend to use the words 'global' and 'analytic' to define these two methods of cognitive processing.

Spotlight on global learners

Global learners perceive material in a holistic manner. They may feel the need to have all the

'Since I learned about the global–analytic model, I find myself noticing how people react in different situations. It has become easier to spot particular behaviour and accept that not all the students cognitively process information in the same way. Rather than a difficulty, I have found it a welcome challenge – as reacting to students' needs is one of the most fulfilling parts of teaching.'

A teacher

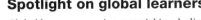

grammar in English presented at one time. Global learners will generally remember the whole experience rather than the details. They enjoy working in groups, but are relationship-oriented and need to feel comfortable with their team members – if they have to work in a group in which they are truly uncomfortable, they will have problems completing the task. Motivation tends to be extrinsic, originating with a desire to please others. Global learners generally value feelings over facts, causing them to make emotional rather than analytic decisions.

This can lead to avoiding competition and taking criticism very personally. It is important for these learners (as for the 'kinaesthetic emotional' type) to relate learning to their personal experiences. They are spontaneous and can work on more than one project at a time, but they like to have an overview. They are much happier when given choices, and tend to live for the moment rather than always planning ahead. They are generally intuitive, perceptive and imaginative.

Spotlight on analytic learners

Analytic learners perceive information in a more detailed and structured way. They tend to remember specifics and may work best alone, as groupwork could be perceived as distracting. This type of learner is generally self-motivated and tends towards intrinsic motivation. They are more task-oriented when working in a group, and make sure that the task is in the forefront.

Facts are more important for them than feelings, and getting the job done often takes priority over socialising and relationships. They have an easier time than global learners do when faced with criticism and can disassociate from it. In some cases, they dismiss the criticism by just assuming the person expressing it is wrong.

Spotlight on global teachers

Global teachers will most likely give general goals to learners rather than specific ones. For example, they may tell learners that they will learn to write 'longer pieces of writing', rather than laying out exactly which types of pieces these will be or even giving a word count. They tend to give concrete examples when explaining concepts, as well as using more personal anecdotes to help get the ideas across.

They encourage their learners to use the 'discovery' or inductive method, allowing them to discover the language through their own observations. They value a student-centred classroom and plan groupwork activities. The social learning environment is of great importance to these teachers, and cooperative learning activities in which learners depend on and help each other may be commonplace.

They may have a plan for themselves but remain somewhat flexible if necessary, in order to make sure their learners have got as much as they could from a topic and are ready to move on to the next. Spontaneity often has a place in the global teacher's classroom and it could happen that they change their lesson plan at the last minute to include a new idea or current topic. They do not generally make use of L1/L2 equivalents but prefer to explain everything in L2.

Spotlight on analytic teachers

Analytic teachers tend to give specific goals of what exactly they expect from their learners. They may discuss language features out of context, and put more emphasis on reflection and analytical thinking. They prefer the deductive approach, in which the learners are presented first with grammar rules and then given drills or other exercises to practise. They may put more emphasis on accuracy and correct factual information than on style, unless they feel it is related directly to the task at hand.

Analytic teachers will avoid giving 'main ideas' but will concentrate on the details. Their plan is carefully structured and adhered to and analytic teachers may also hand it out to learners or tell them at the beginning of the lesson exactly what is going to be covered. Analytic teachers prefer when learners work individually, and may be fond of problem-solving activities which involve reflective and deductive thinking. They will also encourage their learners to judge their own learning rather than rely on peer correction. There will most likely be more use of L1/L2 equivalents, as well. [36]

When looking at the characteristics of global and analytical learning, it is necessary to avoid labelling learners as belonging to one or the other. Witkin himself said in one of his early works that *'the field dependence-independence dimension is a continuous one, most persons falling between these two extremes'.* [37]

We should bear in mind that we are looking here at *tendencies* of learners – understanding that some strategies or methods may be more comfortable for some than others is the point of this book. Learners who can move easily from analytic to global concepts will normally experience a smooth path when it comes to learning. For those who have more difficulty doing this, understanding how to help them is the key to teaching a diverse group of learners.

Important for both teachers *and* learners is to be aware of their own styles in order to make use of their strengths, and to discover why problems may have arisen in specific situations. In addition, knowledge of the different cognitive processing strategies of others can help us to be more tolerant. We can also begin to learn new strategies which may help us when we feel overwhelmed and unable to cope.

Mind Organisation

'It was really interesting to see the way each of us in my team approach tasks. It made things go much more smoothly when I understood the style each person had.'

A manager in an adult education course

The research of Anthony Gregorc [38] provides educators with practical insights into how our students perceive and process or organise their worlds. Gregorc classified perceptional channels as being either 'abstract' or 'concrete'. He defined *abstract* perception as considering the theoretical meaning of received information and *concrete* perception as taking in information through feelings and sensory paths. Once learners have perceived information, they then go on to organise or process it. Gregorc called these methods 'sequential' and 'random'. Using these four measures, he created his Style Delineator – a self-analysis tool designed to assess a person's perceptual and ordering abilities. Depending where people found themselves within the grid, they were categorised into a particular style.

April Bowie (1997) [39] began her research by working with adolescents. Like Gregorc, she developed a self-assessment tool to determine how people learned best – the Mind Organisation Index – and then used the information she obtained to aid learners in their classrooms and in independent work. As the basis for this model also begins with the perception of material, it is important to understand how this is understood in the Bowie model.

Perceiving Both Bowie and Gegoric explore the ways we perceive information: concretely and abstractly. As mentioned above, the 'concrete perception' ability engages our physical senses as well as our feelings and emotions. The 'abstract perception' ability engages our thought processes and our abilities to theorise.

- Learners who perceive **concretely** prefer to absorb information through the senses of sight, smell, touch, taste and hearing. These learners tend to deal with facts, as well as the mechanical or technical details of a task, rather than the underlying concepts or philosophy behind it. They are not comfortable with ambiguity or hazy situations.
- Learners who perceive **abstractly** prefer to tap into their imaginations and intuitive abilities. Those who tend to think abstractly have an easier time perceiving that which is invisible to the physical senses. They focus on concepts, ideas and philosophies. They are skilled at understanding and visualising abstract and theoretical concepts and ideas.

Organising The terms 'systematic' (putting things into sequence and working step-by-step) and 'non-systematic' (organising in a more random or non-linear fashion) relate to our ways of processing or organising information. Gregorc and Bowie both put the organisation of information into two categories. Once the information has been perceived, either concretely or abstractly, we then tend to find a way to make sense of it by organising it *systematically* in a logical order, or having a more fluid approach and dealing with it *non-systematically*. When we use a systematic system we call on our abilities to structure. When we use a non-systematic approach we make use of our abilities to be spontaneous.

- Learners who organise **systematically** prefer a step-by-step approach to learning. These learners are methodical and like to follow exact steps and instructions. They are detailed and exact workers, and may become confused if they receive too much information at one time or have to move quickly from one topic to another.
- Learners who organise **non-systematically** tend to store the information they receive in large chunks. They are more spontaneous thinkers and form concepts tangentially. They can move between ideas or topics easily, and can make associations between different ideas as they don't tend to put items into specific categories in the way the more systematic learners do.

When we look at the combinations of perception and organisation of information, we get four distinct styles. Most people have one strong style and at least one other which is a 'back-up' style and which they can also use to achieve their goals. There is generally one style they tend to use *most* and one which they are *least* likely to use, although most people can demonstrate characteristics from all styles at one time or another, depending on the task or the situation they are in. Learning to stretch out of one's most comfortable style, in order to make use of strategies used by the other styles, can help learners enormously, and is a goal of making them aware of not only their dominant style but also the other three.

Bowie [40] has given these four learning styles the following names:

- Those who perceive information through their five senses and organise it systematically, she called **Power Planners**.
- Those who also perceive through their senses but organise it non-systematically, she has named **Radical Reformers**.
- Those who perceive information in an abstract manner or through their feelings and organise it systematically were given the term **Expert Investigators**.
- Those who also perceive through abstract thoughts or feelings but organise it non-systematically are called **Flexible Friends**.

These styles have distinctive characteristics and can be laid out as in the quadrants below:

'As I was answering these questions, I came to the realisation that I would have answered them differently a few years ago. This made me realise how my style has evolved.'

A teacher trainer

Spotlight on Power Planner learners

The Power Planner learner is organised and punctual. [41] This person tends to be dependable and, as the name implies, plans ahead. The Power Planner may also be a perfectionist, so it may take them more time to finish a piece of work as they want to make sure it is perfect. They are also hard-working, practical and detail-oriented. Power Planners are not happy with constant change and like to know exactly what is expected of them. When working in groups, they tend to take over the role of leader and like to organise things so that the job gets done. They are task-oriented and prefer to spend little time making small talk if possible. Therefore they need rules and clear instructions as well as an organised environment. They generally prefer hands-on learning, practical information and specific examples. Defined targets can help them to organise themselves.

They admire teachers who are structured and organised.

Spotlight on Expert Investigator learners

'My favourite teacher was really an expert in his field. I learned so much from him.'

A learner

The Expert Investigator learners are logical and systematic. [42] Sensible ideas and theories make sense to them and they are generally objective, rational and leave emotions out of their approach to both learning and how they deal with other people. They enjoy doing research and may spend a great deal of time at it. They are extremely thorough and exact so often make excellent proof-readers. However, they can also be sceptical and need all the facts in order to make sense of information they are given, so they tend to find out as much as they can about a particular topic before coming to a decision. They rely on abstract ideas as well as logical arguments, and like to use reason and their intellect to solve problems.

They especially admire teachers who they consider to be experts in their fields.

Spotlight on Flexible Friend learners

The Flexible Friend learner, as the name implies, can be defined as a 'people person'. [43] They are creative and imaginative, but also take things more personally as they can be quite sensitive. This sensitivity is also apparent in their dealings with others, as they tend to be compassionate and emphathetic towards others. They are generally quite spontaneous and also flexible so they adapt to change quite well. Their enthusiasm is often demonstrated openly and they may also be quite idealistic. They value personalised learning and try to have friendly relationships with others whenever possible. In a group, they are more relationship-oriented than task-oriented and may take time at the beginning to get to know those they are working with. They are good friends and listeners, as they understand or at least sympathise with the emotions and feelings of others. Like the global learners, they tend to make decisions with their hearts rather than their heads, and they let their intuition guide them.

They appreciate teachers who show genuine interest in them as people and who try to create a caring atmosphere in the classroom.

Spotlight on Radical Reformer learners

'I love it that my teacher lets us come up with interesting ways to do homework. I spend time finding cartoons or laying it out because it is fun and challenging and never boring.'

A learner

The Radical Reformer learners are risk-takers, adventurous and curious learners. [44] They also rely on their intuition to solve problems but are more competitive than Flexible Friends. They exhibit creativity and value uniqueness, and are especially talented at thinking up unusual and creative ideas and solutions. Some of these characteristics come from their strong will and the fact that they thrive on change. They are generally able to do many things at one time and can be very persuasive and inspiring to others. They use real-world experiences to learn and are the types of learners who especially value authentic materials. They often work in a messy or disorganised environment but they always know where everything is. They are not happy if someone else tries to organise their work space.

They value teachers who respect them as people for their individuality and creative ideas.

Spotlight on Power Planner teachers

The Power Planner teachers set out a plan (much like the analytic teacher) and follow it carefully. While planning, these teachers may make notes as to how long individual activities will take and do their best to keep to this schedule. Their desk is well-organised and they don't have to spend time searching for materials, as they have already made sure they have everything they need. They generally put a lot of effort into preparing handouts and proof-read them to make sure they are perfect. They give exact instructions to their learners and expect these instructions to be followed. They may not be happy working in a staffroom as they prefer a quieter place to work. It is important for them to be able to stay with a plan and keep distractions to a minimum.

Spotlight on Expert Investigator teachers

The Expert Investigator teacher puts a great deal of time into preparation of materials. As Expert Investigators value research highly, people with this teaching style will also spend much time and energy looking for data and information and meticulously preparing for a class. However, their desk may be less organised than the Power Planner, as they are more abstract in their thinking and may become distracted by ideas and theories as they continue to search for materials or information they feel is important. They welcome difficult or complicated questions from learners as they often have a great deal of knowledge at hand, but also relish the idea of finding out as much as they can about a topic and conveying their knowledge to learners. In language classrooms, they generally spend time explaining grammar rules and tend to use drills to consolidate material. It is important to them to feel that they are experts in any field they tackle and are generally willing to invest the time necessary to find out all there is to know about a topic.

Spotlight on Flexible Friend teachers

The Flexible Friend teacher is truly interested in the learners and will take time to get to know them. They may build in activities in which learners talk or write about themselves. They also tell personal stories and place value on sharing feelings, emotions and also ideas, much in the same way a global teacher does. They will listen to learners and try to find solutions to problems if possible. They spend time in the staffroom if the atmsophere there is comfortable. They also help other colleagues whenever possible, and especially enjoy cooperative teaching ideas or other methods in which learners work together in harmonious groups. It is important for them to teach in a classroom where everyone gets along, and they do their best to create this type of atmosphere.

Spotlight on Radical Reformer teachers

The Radical Reformer teacher often looks for new methods or ideas for instruction as well as ways to encourage creativity and innovation among their learners. As they prefer to use their own instincts to solve problems, they may not be happy sticking to a coursebook and will bring in lots of ideas of their own. Doing the same thing over and over is not very interesting for them, so they might try to find unusual ways to teach the basics. They value real-life experience so may look for excursions to take their classes on. As they also enjoy having a certain amount of freedom in their lives, they may not be happy working towards goals set by others. They also like to be in leadership positions, much like the Power Planners, however they tend to be more open and verbal about this. They value change and can be inspirational as colleagues or teachers – it is important to them to provide a certain amount of surprise in the classroom and have the freedom to make choices on their own as to how to work with learners.

A certain amount of overlap will be found between the teaching styles in the Mind Organisation model and the other two models:

- Both the Power Planner and the Expert Investigator perceive information abstractly, so they share certain characteristics with the analytic teacher. They prefer structure and planning although their methods of organisation will differ, setting them apart from the analytical, cognitive processing used in the Global–Analytic model.
- Both the Flexible Friend and the Radical Reformer perceive more concretely, meaning that they share certain tendencies with the global teachers. Again, their organisation of the information will determine how they go about doing tasks and may differ again from the cognitive processing model.

The Mind Organisation model differs from the first two in that it looks more carefully at behavioural tendencies. When we analyse learners or teachers using it, we often find a somewhat more complete picture, as it deals with the aspects of both perception and organisation of the material, whereas the VAK model deals only with sensory perception and the Global–Analytic model looks at cognitive processing but not necessarily perception.

The model also gives both learners and teachers the chance to see not only their *strong* style but their *second* or back-up style as well. Depending on where they fall on the scale of either perception or organisation, one of the models using the same criteria will be their back-up model. For example, a Power Planner's back-up model will be either the Radical Reformer or the Expert Investigator – depending on how they *perceive* and how they *organise* information.

Spotlight on success

Styles and their influence on us can be looked at through successive layers. The outermost layer would be the perceptive channels that people use to make sense of the world around them. This refers to the modalities identified by Barbe and Swassing which are used for acquiring and storing information [45]. As Bowie points out: *'individuals use all three modalities (vision, audition and kinesthesia) for learning; however, they do not use all three equally. Most rely on a dominant preference or stength.'* [46]

Moving on to the next layer, we would consider the cognitive abilities suggested by Witkin [47], whose work dealt with using either field-dependent (global) or field-independent (analytic) methods of processing information. This processing would take place *after* the information has been perceived and stored according to one of the modalities mentioned above.

Finally, coming to the innermost core, we can look at the mind organisation categories. Here, two different aspects are combined, perception of the world around us using concrete or abstract methods, and then organising the information in either a systematic or non-systematic fashion. The resulting category of the four types determined by the Mind Organisation Index [48] gives us another insight into learners: how they behave, the strategies they use, and ideas on helping them to stretch out of their styles to give them the coping strategies they need to be successful.

These characteristics, and how they relate to the three different models, are offered here to provide insight into the way learners approach learning and how teachers can aid them. There is always a chance of overlap of course, but, as mentioned earlier, stress situations generally cause people to rely on the style in which they are most 'at home'.

It is important for both teachers *and* learners to be aware of their *own* styles in order to make use of their strengths, and to discover why problems may have arisen in specific situations. In addition, knowledge of the different cognitive processing strategies of *others* can help us to be more tolerant. We can also begin to learn new strategies which may help us when we feel overwhelmed and unable to cope.

Learning to concentrate on how we learn, rather than what we learn, can be regarded as a first step to life-long learning and as a major factor of motivation – and success!

'I was finally successful in learning a foreign language when I realised I needed to look words up in the dictionary and write down the information I needed to learn so that I could see it.'

The visual learner quoted on page 6, who is also the author of this book

Bibliography

1   Barbe, W B and Swassing, R H *Teaching through modality strengths: Concepts and practices* Zaner-Bloser Inc. 1979

2   Witkin, H A and Goodenough, D R *Cognitive Styles: Essence and Origins* International Universities Press 1981

3   Bowie, A *Mind Organisation* The Learning Styles Institute 1997

4   Harmer, J *The Practice of English Language Teaching* Longman 2007

5   Guild, P B and Garger, S *Marching to Different Drummers* Association for Supervision and Curriculum Development (ASCD) 1998

6   Gregorc, A *An Adult's Guide to Style* Gregorc Associates 1982

7   Dunn, R, Dunn, K and Price, G E *Learning Style Inventory* Price Systems 1975

8   Barbe, W B and Swassing, R H op. cit.

9   Bandler, R and Grinder, J *Frogs into Princes* Real People Press 1979

10 Grinder, M *Righting the Educational Conveyor Belt* Metamorphous Press 1991

11 Barbe, W B and Swassing, R H op. cit.

12 Rosenberg, M 'Learning and Styles: Learner-Differentiated Approaches and Methods' In *Looking at Learning* Waxman 2011

13 Woodward, T *Planning Lessons and Courses* CUP 2001

14 Keefe, J W 'Learning styles: an overview' In Keefe, J S (Ed) *Student learning styles: diagnosing and prescribing problems* Reston National Association of Secondary School Principles 1979 – quote taken from König, M E *Theory of learning styles and practical applications* Grin Verlag Norderstedt 2005

15 Reid, J *Learning Styles in the ESL/EFL Classroom* Heinle and Heinle 1995 – quote taken from Roche, T *Investigating Learning Style in the Foreign Language Classroom* Langenscheidt 2006

16 Kinsella, K 'Understanding and empowering diverse learners in the ESL classroom' In Reid, J *Learning Styles in the ESL/EFL Classroom* Heinle and Heinle 1995 – quote taken from Roche, T *Investigating Learning Style in the Foreign Language Classroom* Langenscheidt 2006

17 Cohen, A 'Focus on the Language Learner: Styles, Strategies and Motivation' In Schmitt N (Ed) *An Introduction to Applied Linguistics* Hodder Education 2002

18 Dunn, R and Dunn, K *The Complete Guide to the Learning Styles* Inservice System Allyn and Bacon 1999

19 Roche, T *Investigating Learning Style in the Foreign Language Classroom* Langenscheidt 2006

20 Roche, T ibid.

21 Harmer, J op. cit.

22 Rosenberg, M op. cit.

23 Rosenberg, M ibid.

24 Revell, J and Norman, S *In Your Hands: NLP in ELT* Saffire Press 1997

25 Dörnyei, Z *Motivational Strategies in the Language Classroom* CUP 2001

26 Dörnyei, Z ibid.

27 Dörnyei, Z ibid.

28 Rosenberg, M 'The How of Thinking: The Secrets of Neuro-Linguistic Programming' *Analytic Teaching, The Community of Enquiry Journal* 20 (2) Viterbo University 2000

29 Grinder, M op. cit.

30 O'Connor, H and Seymour, J *Introducing Neuro-Linguistic Programming* Mandala 1990

31 O'Connor, H and Seymour, J ibid.

32 O'Connor, H and Seymour, J ibid.

33 http://www.nobelprize.org/educational/medicine/split-brain/background.html 15.02.2012 11.40am

34 http://neuroarts.org/pdf/musiclanguage.pdf 17.27

35 Witkin, H A and Goodenough, D R op. cit.

36 Roche, T op. cit.

37 Witkin, H A 'A cognitive approach to cross-cultural research' *International Journal of Psychology* 2 (4) 1967

38 Gregorc, A op. cit.

39 Bowie, A op. cit.

40 Bowie, A ibid.

41 Bowie, A ibid.

42 Bowie, A ibid.

43 Bowie, A ibid.

44 Bowie, A ibid.

45 Barbe, W B and Swassing, R H op. cit.

46 Bowie, A *Adolescent Self Perceptions of Learning Styles: A Qualitative Study*, Master's Thesis, Antioch University, Seattle 1998

47 Witkin, H A and Goodenough, D R op. cit.

48 Bowie, A op. cit.

Spotlight on learning styles has shed light on three specific learning style models and their importance for successful teaching and learning. Now that the fundamentals have been explored, we can begin to take action and apply this knowledge.

Spotlight on strategies leads both you the teacher, as well as your learners, on a journey of discovery. By doing the Checklists and then checking your answers against the Keys, you can begin to put together your individual learning profile. Examining the characteristics – and the strategies both for learning and for teaching suggested for each model – will offer you further insight into your unique way of processing information and reflecting on what you do in order to learn. As this is a constant process, becoming aware of your style will allow you to observe yourself and your learners, gaining knowledge as you progress on each step of the way.

The VAK model of multi-sensory instruction has become part of the curricula for a number of teacher training programmes worldwide. This type of teaching was used successfully with younger children by educators such as Dr Maria Montessori, but there is no reason why this type of teaching cannot continue with older and adult learners. Our styles are set early on but we learn to adapt as we get older, and most learners would agree that being comfortable in a class is motivating and provides a reason to go come for more and continue taking an active part.

The Global–Analytic model deals with the cognitive processing of information. As it is completely independent from the VAK model, it adds another layer to the learning style profile and may clarify why certain aspects of the learning process are easier for some learners than for others. The activities help us to offer strategies to learners who have been feeling overwhelmed – due to materials being presented in a way they were having trouble grasping. Showing them *alternatives* can set the basis for more self-confidence, leading to better performance and creating a cycle of success rather than failure.

The Mind Organisation model helps us to understand our own behaviour as well as the behaviour of our learners, and gives insight into both – and the resulting actions that manifest themselves in the classroom. For teachers, and for the learners themselves, finding out how they approach tasks can be enlightening. Understanding *why* someone needs a particular 'method' can help us to be more tolerant towards those who are very different.

These, then, are the directions in which we shall be going in Part B.

The activities

The activities in Chapters Two, Three and Four are presented in such a way as to make them user-friendly and easy to implement in a variety of teaching situations:

Strategy

The specific strategies inherent in each individual activity are very briefly described, to explain at a glance the objectives of the activity.

Spotlight on style

The individual styles for which the activities have been designed are marked clearly, while the final activities in each chapter have elements of *all* the styles within each model.

Spotlight on language

This will help you in planning your lessons or prepare you for practising particular lexis or grammar.

Set-up

Some activities require a certain amount of preparation or materials. You will see immediately if you need to bring something with you, to photocopy and cut up materials for the learners, or prepare questions or topics before the lesson.

Steps

The procedure for each activity is spelled out 'step by step'. Following the icon ▼, you will find suggestions for extending the activities. These can include homework, portfolio work, stretching the activity to appeal to other learner types, or reviewing what has been accomplished.

Style spectrum

A Spectrum is provided for every activity and shows the aspects of the activity with regard to *other* learner styles. Beyond its principal focus, it can be helpful to see what makes an activity more diverse – in order to include and appeal to learners of other styles. For example:

- For the **VAK** chapter, aspects of the activities which the other VAK learner types would find appealing are listed, as well as the elements for global or analytic learners.
- In the **Global–Analytic** chapter, the three basic VAK styles are mentioned, as well as the *other* global/analytic learner type (the one *not* under the spotlight) – except in the mixed section, where both the global *and* analytic elements are pointed out.
- For the **Mind Organisation** chapter, the Spectrum includes only the Mind Organisation styles, as both *perception* and *processing* are incorporated already within the model.

It is important to remember that these are *general* comments regarding these learner types and apply to *general* teaching and learning situations – although the comments in the Spectrum directly relate to the activity which they describe.

The outcomes

It is also important to bear in mind that learners may react in different ways to an activity, and the outcome could be different from what you are expecting. For example:

- Some learners may want to make notes in order to solve the logic puzzles which are planned as auditory activities, or they may connect a particular sentence with a particular person and remember things in that way, rather than concentrating solely on what they have heard.
- In some of the mixed activities, such as the guessing game *Animal, vegetable, mineral*, some learners may tend to rely more heavily on adjectives that describe what something looks like, while others may go for the purpose of the item or the feeling it gives them.
- There are several activities dealing with a similar topic, such as 'planning a trip'. However, these have been specifically designed in such a way that the methods used by the learners – and the outcomes – are different.

Some of the activities were discovered in professional development seminars or in other published materials, and have been adapted to suit the learning styles and then extensively tried and tested – with varying outcomes. (Acknowledgements have been given when the sources were clear but, in some cases, it has not been possible to identify the original inspiration for the activities.)

The main premise of *Spotlight on Learning Styles* and the activities that follow is to engage the learners so that they actually 'forget' they are speaking a foreign language.

When learners become involved in solving a puzzle, when they work together to achieve an aim or just have fun playing a game, when they respond to strategies which make them feel comfortable because they appeal to their particular strengths … they have the chance to 'lose themselves' and react spontaneously.

The next step

Chapter One, opposite, gives you the opportunity to know your own style and the styles of your learners – by means of three checklists (which can be conducted, if necessary, in the learners' mother tongue).

Doing these three questionnaires – and discussing the characteristics of the styles and then reflecting on the learner and teacher strategies suggested – should allow you to get off to a flying start.

Chapter One

Spotlight on strategies

The first chapter focuses on *how* we and our students learn.
We become aware of our preferred learning styles and those of our learners,
and discover strategies for both learning and teaching.

Visual, Auditory and Kinaesthetic

Checklist, Key and Learner strategies

Global–Analytic

Checklist, Key and Learner strategies

Mind Organisation

Index, Key and Learner strategies

Teacher strategies

VAK

Checklist

Tick the statements which are usually true for you. Remember there are no right or wrong answers.

- ☐ **1** I like to hear new material explained.
- ☐ **2** I learn by making personal connections to the material.
- ☐ **3** Getting handouts is important for me.
- ☐ **4** I like to move around in the classroom.
- ☐ **5** I need to feel comfortable with others in the group.
- ☐ **6** I like using different colours or highlighters.
- ☐ **7** I need to repeat the material out loud.
- ☐ **8** I need to try things out in order to learn them.
- ☐ **9** I enjoy reading, going to the cinema or watching TV.
- ☐ **10** I like to have music in the background.
- ☐ **11** I like a classroom that feels cosy and friendly.
- ☐ **12** I do a lot of sports.
- ☐ **13** Ideas come to me when I am exercising, walking or moving about.
- ☐ **14** I enjoy discussions with classmates or colleagues.
- ☐ **15** I like a classroom which is decorated with posters, pictures and so on.
- ☐ **16** My workspace has photos of family and friends.
- ☐ **17** I learn well through hearing stories.

- ☐ **18** I tend to forget things I haven't written down.
- ☐ **19** My workspace has a comfortable chair and enough room to move about.
- ☐ **20** I remember best when material has an emotional connection for me.
- ☐ **21** I remember things I have seen.
- ☐ **22** People and situations trigger emotions for me.
- ☐ **23** I rarely take notes during lectures.
- ☐ **24** I often play with small objects, such as keys or coins, while learning.
- ☐ **25** I can imitate other people's voices well.
- ☐ **26** I learn best from a teacher or person I like.
- ☐ **27** I like to have 'active' holidays.
- ☐ **28** I need to write words down in order to make sure they are spelled correctly.
- ☐ **29** Colours are important to me.
- ☐ **30** I enjoy listening to the radio.
- ☐ **31** I don't like to sit for a long period of time without moving.
- ☐ **32** Having several close friends is very important for me.

Key

Circle the numbers you ticked:

Visual	**Auditory**	**Kinaesthetic emotional**	**Kinaesthetic motoric**
3, 6, 9, 15, 18, 21, 28, 29	1, 7, 10, 14, 17, 23, 25, 30	2, 5, 11, 16, 20, 22, 26, 32	4, 8, 12, 13, 19, 24, 27, 31

Your preference profile
Put the number of circles in the boxes:

☐ Visual   ☐ Auditory   ☐ Kinaesthetic emotional (KE)   ☐ Kinaesthetic motoric (KM)

Now fill in this grid demonstrating your preference profile.
Colour in the number of fields – the number of sentences you circled above – to better visualise your profile.

8				
7				
6				
5				
4				
3				
2				
1				
	V	**A**	**KE**	**KM**

Discussion points:
- Did you tick more answers for one type than another, or did you tick the same number for several types?
- Do you agree with the answers?
- How did you judge yourself *before* doing this survey? Was it the same or different?

Points to remember:
The actual number in each of the modalities is not important – it is the relation *between* the points that indicates learning style. Therefore, a significantly higher number in one area will indicate strength in that area, as compared to another area with a lower number of points.

VAK

Learner strategies

If you are a Visual learner:

- Use colours and highlighters.
- Write down things that you need to learn.
- Organise things in a way that makes most sense to you.
- Create images of material you need to learn.
- Make use of graphic organisers or mind-maps.

Stretching out of your comfort zone / learning to cope:

- Don't forget to rearrange material you have to learn and learn it again in a different order.
- You may need to spend time:
  - practising pronunciation;
  - listening carefully and modelling language patterns and their melodies;
  - learning to listen actively.

If you are an Auditory learner:

- Repeat material aloud to yourself or imagine that you hear a voice repeating it.
- Practise for tests with an imaginary person.
- Study out loud with friends or classmates.
- Participate orally in class.
- Listen carefully.
- Record material and read along while listening to it.

Stretching out of your comfort zone / learning to cope:

- Don't forget to write material down and learn it again visually.
- You may need to spend time:
  - practising handwriting;
  - learning to take notes;
  - learning to visualise.

If you are a Kinaesthetic emotional learner:

- Find personal connections to the material.
- Study in a place in which you feel comfortable.
- Create positive feelings about learning.
- Find personal reasons for learning a subject.
- Study in a group of people you feel like to be with.

Stretching out of your comfort zone / learning to cope:

- Don't forget that you need to learn how to separate your emotions from the learning situation.
- You may need to spend time:
  - learning to work with everyone;
  - learning to use facts;
  - distancing yourself from problems and keeping them from distracting you.

If you are a Kinaesthetic motoric learner:

- Try information out for yourself.
- Take frequent breaks.
- Hold small objects (keys, ball, pen, etc) while learning.
- Make flashcards and practise with them.
- Volunteer for roleplays in the classroom.
- Walk about while learning.

Stretching out of your comfort zone / learning to cope:

- Don't forget to write down anything that you have learned while walking about, as you need this for your visual memory.
- You may need to spend time:
  - practising handwriting;
  - learning to sit still;
  - learning not to play with small objects in class.

Notes

Global–Analytic

Checklist

Tick the statements which are most like you. Then circle the numbers you chose under the Global and Analytic categories below, adding up the circles underneath. Remember there are no right or wrong answers.

☐ **1** I prefer to have an overview, but not all the details, of a lesson or material I have to learn before I start.

☐ **2** I normally prefer to finish one project before beginning another.

☐ **3** I usually like to know what exactly a course will cover.

☐ **4** I like to please other people, and their opinions are important to me.

☐ **5** I usually need to relate what I am learning to my own experiences and life.

☐ **6** I am generally self-motivated.

☐ **7** I usually take a non-emotional approach to learning.

☐ **8** I usually prefer to work in a group, especially one in which I like other people.

☐ **9** I would describe myself as being intuitive, perceptive and imaginative.

☐ **10** I often prefer to work alone.

☐ **11** I would describe myself as being logical and rational.

☐ **12** I usually prefer to work step-by-step.

☐ **13** I prefer to remain flexible, and can easily go from one point or topic to another.

☐ **14** I often work on more than one project at a time.

☐ **15** I usually focus on the details of a lesson or material I have to learn.

☐ **16** I am content to go with the flow.

☐ **17** I don't usually get personally involved with the other members of a group I work with.

☐ **18** I generally feel hurt when other people criticise me or my work.

☐ **19** I usually remember the whole experience rather than the details.

☐ **20** I can usually take criticism in a non-emotional way.

☐ **21** I usually make decisions based on emotions and feelings.

☐ **22** I tend to remember details of things I have learned or experienced.

☐ **23** I normally make decisions based on facts and logic.

☐ **24** I usually like to have choices about how to complete a task.

☐ **25** I sometimes overlook details.

☐ **26** I generally stay on task in a group.

☐ **27** I usually like to follow specific procedures to complete a task.

☐ **28** I am spontaneous.

☐ **29** I usually like to plan for the future.

☐ **30** I often get personally involved with the other members of a group I work with.

Key

Global
1, 4, 5, 8, 9, 13, 14, 16, 18, 19, 21, 24, 25, 28, 30

Analytic
2, 3, 6, 7, 10, 11, 12, 15, 17, 20, 22, 23, 26, 27, 29

Your preference profile

☐ Global   ☐ Analytic   Now mark the number of circles on this continuum – to better visualise your profile.

| G | 15 14 13 12 11 10 9 8 7 6 5 4 3 2 1 | 1 2 3 4 5 6 7 8 9 10 11 12 13 14 15 | A |

Discussion points:
- Did you come out strongly on one side of the centre line or the other, or were you more in the middle?
- Do you think that you use both global and analytic abilities, depending on the task at hand?
- How did you judge yourself *before* doing this survey? Was it the same or different?

Points to remember:
This checklist is designed to see if you are more 'global' or more 'analytic', or if you use both strategies equally – to see where you fall on the continuum. The more points you have in one category, the more likely you are to have those characteristics. Most people tend to fall somewhere in the middle, although some are further to one side than the other. It is helpful to know where your tendencies are in order to discover for yourself how you can develop successful learning strategies.

Remember that this can also be dependent on outside influences and particular situations. So observe yourself in different scenarios – to see if these tendencies are common, or specific to what you are doing.

Global–Analytic

Learner strategies

If you are a Global learner:

- Find ways to relate the material to your life and make associations to it.
- Work in groups in which you are comfortable.
- Ask for help if you need it.
- Discover how you can best organise your material and develop your own organisational system.
- Ask for an overview.
- Use mind-maps to help you remember.
- Find out what the objectives are in a course so that you know what is expected of you.
- Find ways to use your creativity and imagination.
- Use the whole picture to determine the details.
- Create your own system of learning through trial and error.

Stretching out of your comfort zone / learning to cope:

- Don't forget to make a list of things you need to do.
- You may need to:
  - practise prioritising tasks and not try to do everything at once;
  - learn basic organisational techniques to keep from becoming overwhelmed;
  - understand when 'structure' is more important to achieve goals than spontaneity and flexibility;
  - learn how to make rules and guidelines work for you;
  - find ways to motivate yourself;
  - try to take criticism less emotionally, and learn from it.

If you are an Analytic learner:

- Link the details together to make a big picture.
- Work alone if you need to.
- Set goals for yourself.
- Record your progress.
- Work on one thing at a time.
- Make sure you know exactly what is expected of you regarding procedures and rules.
- Find out where you can get the facts or details you need.
- Organise your materials or learning in a step-by-step way.
- Determine exactly what the task is that you need to complete.
- Set out your own plan for the future.

Stretching out of your comfort zone / learning to cope:

- Don't forget to keep your eye on the overall picture and not only on the individual parts.
- You may need to:
  - learn when the final goal is more important than getting distracted by details you feel you have not yet conquered;
  - find out when you can more easily accept alternative ideas and let go of fixed ones;
  - understand when flexibility and spontaneity are more important in achieving goals than structure;
  - learn how to adapt to groupwork when team members have different styles from you;
  - take a step back from the details to see the whole picture;
  - learn to 'go with the flow' if plans suddenly change.

Notes

Mind Organisation

Index

The Index includes ten statements – with four options for each statement. Read each statement and decide how it refers to you. Give *four* points to the option most important to you, *three* points to the one you prefer next, *two* to the next one, and *one* point to the option you prefer least. No two statements in a set can have the same number of points. There are no wrong answers.

4 = most like me
3 = often like me
2 = sometimes like me
1 = least like me

1 My approach to learning

When beginning a task or assignment …

- **A** I make sure I have clear instructions I can follow.
- **B** I prefer to have detailed and explicit information about the task.
- **C** I am usually eager to begin the task, sometimes before reading or listening to all of the directions.
- **D** I need to know that I will have support from someone else if I don't understand.

2 My learning style

I learn best …

- **A** by using a step-by-step approach.
- **B** when I have the time to think to myself about details, facts and logical explanations.
- **C** from real-life experiences and a 'hands-on' approach.
- **D** when I can talk to others and relate the lesson to my life.

3 My approach to problem solving

When I solve a problem …

- **A** I look for solutions that are logical, simple and sensible.
- **B** I take my time to think about it.
- **C** I use my instincts to come up with my own creative solution.
- **D** I share and discuss solutions with friends, family members and colleagues.

4 My schedule

- **A** I prefer to have the same schedule or routine each day.
- **B** I try to have sufficient time to do a good job.
- **C** I avoid routines as much as possible.
- **D** I can adapt easily if my plan for the day is interrupted.

5 My work space

- **A** I like to keep my work space neat and organised.
- **B** My work space is usually organised but sometimes gets messy.
- **C** I organise in piles rather than files.
- **D** My work space often looks like a disaster area.

6 My team/groupwork description

In my various roles, I typically serve as the …

- **A** organiser; administrator.
- **B** researcher; critic.
- **C** change-agent; activist.
- **D** morale-builder; mentor.

7 My communication style

When addressing an important issue …

- **A** I am direct, even if it means that I hurt someone's feelings.
- **B** I prefer to have ample time to think about (and perhaps explore) the matter.
- **C** I usually convey my gut reactions.
- **D** I try to be sensitive to other people's feelings.

8 Working in groups

- **A** When I work in groups, I like to stay on task until we get the job done.
- **B** I prefer not to work in groups and would rather work by myself.
- **C** When I work in groups, I am often the leader and my group has an unusual and creative product.
- **D** I enjoy working in a group where I am comfortable.

9 A different point of view

My friends would describe me as …

- **A** loyal, dependable and hard-working.
- **B** sensible and logical.
- **C** adventurous.
- **D** a good listener and an understanding person.

10 My point of view

I would describe myself as …

- **A** a perfectionist.
- **B** inquisitive but sceptical.
- **C** unique and strong-willed.
- **D** imaginative, spontaneous and creative.

Mind Organisation

Key

A = Power Planner   **B** = Expert Investigator   **C** = Radical Reformer   **D** = Flexible Friend

Your preference profile

Add up the points and find your style. Put the total number of points into the boxes.

☐ **A** Power Planner   ☐ **B** Expert Investigator   ☐ **C** Radical Reformer   ☐ **D** Flexible Friend

Look at the radar chart below. Mark your points on the lines corresponding to your style. The lowest number you can get is 10, the highest 40. Now connect the four marks you made – to get a visualisation of your style.

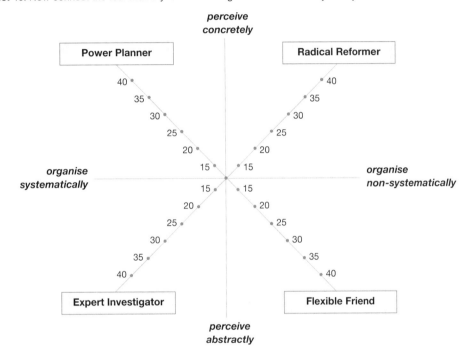

Example:

This is a completed chart, visualising a personal profile.

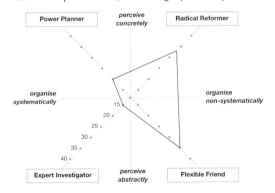

Discussion points:

- Do you have significantly more points in one style than another, or are the points distributed very evenly?
- Do you think that the evaluation of your style is correct?
- How did you judge yourself *before* doing this survey? Was it the same or different?

Points to remember:

Some people have a clear majority of points in one of the four styles, while others may have a more even split. This can depend on the situation that they are in at the time, and they may use different strategies to work on different problems or tasks. It is advisable to observe yourself for a time *after* filling in the Index and notice when you tend to use the characteristics of one of the styles more than another. Sometimes it is necessary to practise stretching to another style to be successful in a particular situation.

Mind Organisation

Learner strategies

If you are a Power Planner:

- Make a checklist and write down exactly what needs to be done first. Tick off items after they are completed.
- Relate what you need to learn to practical situations.
- Make sure that you have exact instructions. You may have to ask your teacher for a specific example so that you know what you have to do.

Stretching out of your comfort zone / learning to cope:

- Don't allow the personalities of your teacher or your classmates to distract you from what you have to do; concentrate on the content.
- You may need to:
  - learn to accept someone else's plan;
  - learn to let someone else lead a group;
  - learn to accept change.

If you are an Expert Investigator:

- Make sure that you have all the information you need or know where to find it in order to complete a task.
- Ensure that you know exactly what is expected of you and what is necessary in order to complete your assignment correctly.
- Ask your teacher if you can have more time in order to reflect on your work if it is necessary. If you are learning at home, make sure you have enough time to complete your assignment in a quiet place without interruptions.

Stretching out of your comfort zone / learning to cope:

- Practise working at home with time limits so that you can learn to work more quickly at school when it is necessary.
- You may need to:
  - learn to be less of a perfectionist;
  - learn to accept other people's opinions;
  - spend more time doing social activities and working with others.

If you are a Flexible Friend:

- Find out who you can ask for help if you need it. This could be your teacher, parents, friends or classmates.
- Create your own comfortable, relaxed learning atmosphere.
- Find personal connections to make things easier to learn.

Stretching out of your comfort zone / learning to cope:

- Find a fun way to organise your learning schedule. Decide what is really most important to do first and make a list for yourself.
- You may need to:
  - concentrate less on personal relationships if they are interfering with your learning goals;
  - learn to look more carefully at details;
  - discover how to make decisions with your head and less with your heart.

If you are a Radical Reformer:

- Find personal and important reasons for yourself to learn and to finish assignments.
- Negotiate with your teacher in order to find different possibilities of finishing your assignments.
- If you are at school, talk with your parents about choosing when and where to learn, as long as your grades are OK.
- Decide for yourself if your strategies are working and, if not, look for a way to change them.

Stretching out of your comfort zone / learning to cope:

- Learn how to set priorities for yourself. Decide what is most important and the order in which you should do things.
- You may need to:
  - learn to concentrate on one project at a time – wait before starting another;
  - keep from making impulsive decisions;
  - learn to fit in, while retaining your sense of individuality.

Notes

Teacher strategies

Visual, Auditiory, Kinaesthetic

Helping Visual learners

- Use colours (coloured chalk, colourful presentation slides and posters; encourage the learners to use colours in their work) – while making sure the colours are used consistently.
- Copy different aspects of language learning onto different coloured paper (eg grammar on yellow, exercises on green, etc).
- Use sketches, diagrams and charts.
- Make use of visual aids (OHTs, posters, video, etc).
- Emphasise important information (eg core information and new material) on separate pages.
- Explain the index card system of learning.
- Teach mind-mapping, and use it to explain material.
- Offer visualisation possibilities in class.
- Put material to be learned above eye level.

Helping them to develop new learning strategies
- Practise speaking clearly and slowly.
- Incorporate listening comprehension exercises.

Helping Auditory learners

- Use dialogues as a teaching technique.
- Make use of classroom discussions.
- Announce the topic (giving an overview at the beginning of the lesson).
- Use metaphors and tell stories.
- Summarise aloud.
- Give examples of what to listen for.
- Speak rhythmically.
- Encourage class discussions.

Helping them to develop new learning strategies
- Prepare clear handouts.
- Write information on the board.

Helping Kinaesthetic motoric learners

- Build movement into lessons.
- Use roleplays.
- Be concrete and specific.
- Make use of physical contact.
- Use manipulatives and realia.
- Make use of the computer.
- Use drama techniques, theatre and mime.
- Re-teach a theoretical concept by using movement or objects.

Helping them to develop new learning strategies
- Use 'quiet time' and seat work.
- Allow the learners time to make notes or just think and reflect.

Helping Kinaesthetic emotional learners

- Create a positive atmosphere in the classroom.
- Make use of humour and fun.
- Show genuine interest in the learners.
- Use groupwork and cooperative learning activities.
- Facilitate creating personal associations to the material.
- Acknowledge the learners' feelings and emotional states.

Helping them to develop new learning strategies
- Be factual.
- Avoid too much personal contact.

Global–Analytic

Helping Global learners

- State the end result.
- Let the learners work in groups.
- Give general overviews of language structures.
- Give summaries and allow time for questions or review.
- Let the learners help you plan your lessons and give input on topics.
- Look after individual learners if necessary, and give them more time if they need it.
- Use a mix of methods.
- Keep presentations of material short.
- Use collaborative activities.
- Make use of movement.
- Praise the learners for their efforts and improvement.

Helping them to develop new learning strategies
- Encourage the learners to prioritise and write lists.
- Teach them to work individually, as well as in groups.

Helping Analytic learners

- Give rules and procedures.
- Concentrate on details.
- Let the learners work on their own.
- Structure material clearly and break it down into chunks.
- Give detailed summaries of what you plan to cover.
- Explain exactly how you expect the learners to proceed.
- Set time limits for all the activities.
- Stay with one topic as long as necessary.
- Supply data, facts and background information.
- Use activities which have a competitive element.
- Keep your classroom and lessons structured.
- Praise the learners for their work and progress.

Helping them to develop new learning strategies
- Encourage the learners to keep the big picture in mind.
- Get them to practise groupwork and to accept the opinions of the others.

Teacher strategies

Mind Organisation

Helping the Power Planner

- Give the learners an exact schedule of what will be covered and when.
- Give written and verbal instructions for assignments, including all the necessary details.
- Make sure the learners know which form (written or oral) output should take when doing groupwork.
- Make use of practical 'hands-on' learning experiences.
- Give specific examples whenever possible.
- Give the learners exact dates when assignments or projects are due, and what exactly is expected for a specific grade. (Avoid statements like *Give it to me whenever you finish it* or *It doesn't matter what colour ink you use*.) Be consistent.
- Give exact feedback when handing back corrected assignments.
- Keep the classroom and the lesson plans organised.
- Give examples of how the learning material can be used in a practical situation.

Helping them to develop new learning strategies

- Encourage the learners to work in cooperative learning groups and to take on new roles (not always being the organiser). Praise their social skills as well as their organisational skills.
- Teach them to practise writing essays by making outlines first so that they can learn creativity through structure.

Helping the Expert Investigator

- Allow your learners enough time to finish an assignment.
- Inform the learners about sources where they can do their own research and find more information.
- Create possibilities in which they can research material on their own.
- Build debates into your lessons – teach the learners how to analyse and consider issues from all sides.
- Try to answer all their questions. (Look up answers for the next class if necessary.) Allow time for their concepts and theories.
- Be consistent with rules, expectations and methods of assessment.
- Don't use emotions when making decisions, especially in situations dealing with classroom management.
- Announce time frames and structure lessons so that the learners have the feeling they know what to expect next.

Helping them to develop new learning strategies

- Teach the learners how to take concise notes and to find and summarise the important parts of the information.
- Get them to learn how to deal with 'concrete' or realistic learning materials and use 'hands-on' projects in a constructive way.

Helping the Flexible Friend

- Create a comfortable, inviting classroom.
- Allow time for the learners' personal stories.
- Encourage them to personalise their binders and books.
- Recognise effort, praising the process and the social skills used, as well as the result.
- Encourage them to ask for help if they need it, and make sure they know who they can ask.
- Use groupwork or learning teams, giving the learners time for discussions with each other.
- Show sensitivity when dealing with topics which are important to them.
- Make your instruction more personal – tell stories, use humour, etc.
- Show the learners that you like them as people.
- Make them see that they are important and that their personal involvement can help others in the world.

Helping them to develop new learning strategies

- Suggest different options for personal organisation and prioritising what they need to do.
- Encourage them to learn how to work with other learners who may not be their friends, or with whom they don't have a personal relationship.

Helping the Radical Reformer

- Don't push the learners into a corner.
- Stress general rules rather than exact regulations – allow the possibility of choices.
- Give the learners the chance to negotiate with you while maintaining your authority.
- Make your lessons interesting and varied – try to avoid always doing what is expected, and change your routine from time to time.
- Create assignments that provide some challenge – give the learners, or encourage them to find, personal reasons for learning the material.
- Encourage leadership qualities in them.
- Create situations in which creative problem-solving strategies are required.
- Use real-life experiences and authentic material when possible.

Helping them to develop new learning strategies

- Suggest organisational strategies, or encourage the learners to find their own unique way of organising the material.
- Encourage them to finish tasks or projects which they have started.

Chapter Two
Visual, Auditory and Kinaesthetic learning styles

The chapter on VAK sensory perception includes differentiated activities
for visual, auditory, kinaesthetic emotional and kinaesthetic motoric learners,
as well as a section of activities which make use of a mix of these styles.

A fuller explanation of how the content of the activities
has been structured is presented on page 28.

Visual

- What have I changed?
- What have we changed?
- What are they wearing?
- Find the shapes
- Putting it together
- I'm looking at something …
- If I fly to the moon …
- Whose line is the longest?

Auditory

- Pass it on!
- Puzzle it out!
- Reconstructing cartoons
- Reconstructing texts
- What's the joke?
- Secret identities
- Let me be your guide
- Jigsaw listening

Kinaesthetic emotional

- Emotional objects
- Positive personalities
- Horoscope
- It's in the cards
- Planning a trip
- Outlines
- Roll a mood
- It makes me feel …

Kinaesthetic motoric

- It's in the bag
- Creating a machine
- Back-writing telephone
- Mime artist
- Acting out adverbs
- Sticky-note body
- This is my knee
- Becoming a statue

Mixed VAK

- Becoming a picture
- Back-to-back drawing
- Memory
- VAK bingo
- Your last holiday
- Look: no mistakes!
- Interesting definitions
- Who went where?
- Run and dictate
- Run and draw

What have I changed?

Strategy
Looking carefully at a partner and noticing what they have changed about their appearance.

Spotlight on style
Visual

Spotlight on language
Clothing; present perfect tense

Steps

- ☐ Pre-teach or revise articles of clothing and verbs.
  For example:
  jumper / cardigan
  trousers / jeans
  roll up / roll down
  button / unbutton
  take off / put on

- ☐ Remind the learners that the present perfect tense is often used to describe actions which took place in the past but have an important result in the present.

- ☐ Put the learners into pairs:
  - ☐ They stand opposite each other.
  - ☐ They look at each other carefully.
  - ☐ They turn away.
  - ☐ They all change something about their appearance.
  - ☐ They turn back again and look at each other.

- ☐ The partners tell each other what has changed.

This can also be done with two pairs working together.

In a whole-class activity, one person can be asked to go out of the room and alter their appearance.
- ☐ You call them back in.
- ☐ You ask the others to say what they have changed about their appearance.

The learners can be asked to write out the changes, or explain in open class the difference between the original situation and the changed one.

Style spectrum
- Speculating aloud is auditory.
- Being aware of others is kinaesthetic emotional.
- Putting on or removing something is kinaesthetic motoric.
- Collaborating is global.
- Pinpointing details is analytic.

What have we changed?

Strategy
Observing changes in the classroom and pointing them out.

Spotlight on style
Visual

Spotlight on language
Classroom items; passive voice; present perfect tense

Steps

- ☐ Ask two volunteer learners to go out of the room.

- ☐ Ask the other learners to move things around.
  For example:
  - ☐ They move items, such as a flipchart.
  - ☐ They move things around on their desks.
  - ☐ They change places.

- ☐ There should be at least six changes.

- ☐ Call the volunteers back in.

- ☐ Tell them to identify and point out what has changed, or has been changed, in the room.

The learners can be asked to write out the changes. They can then compare their papers with a partner to see if they remembered everything – and discuss what they have written down.

A further step would be for the learners to write a text about what has changed (or has been changed) in their schools/home towns/institutions/companies in the last few years.

Style spectrum
- Discussing is auditory.
- Working as a group is kinaesthetic emotional.
- Moving things around is kinaesthetic motoric.
- Seeing the room holistically is global.
- Finding details is analytic.

What are they wearing?

Strategy
Trying to remember what others in the classroom are wearing.

Spotlight on style
Visual

Spotlight on language
Clothing; colours; present progressive tense

Steps

☐ Pre-teach or revise articles of clothing: styles, colours, patterns, etc, without calling attention to what individuals are wearing.

☐ Send half the class out of the room.
  ▫ You write a list of all the people out of the room and give it to those in the classroom.
  ▫ You write a second list of those in the classroom and give it to those outside.

☐ Tell the two groups to write down what they can remember about the clothing of the other group. They should mention each person individually.

☐ When the groups have finished, call those who are outside back in.
  ▫ Each group reads out what they wrote, without mentioning the names.
  ▫ Each person who is being described stands up.

☐ Encourage the learners to make corrections to the clothing they have mentioned after they have read what they have written. For example:
Paula is not wearing a red sweater, she is wearing a blue one.

▼

This can also be used to practise the past progressive tense – by using the same information in a later class. The groups change the tense to the past and read it out. They can also reformulate the corrections:
We thought Paula was wearing … , but she was wearing … .

Style spectrum

- Talking together is auditory.
- Sharing information with others is kinaesthetic emotional.
- Going out of the room is kinaesthetic motoric.
- Guessing is global.
- Correcting details is analytic.

Find the shapes

Strategy
Finding shapes in a drawing.

Spotlight on style
Visual

Spotlight on language
Names of shapes

Set-up

You will need a piece of A3 paper and pens or crayons of different colours.

Steps

☐ Pre-teach or revise the names of shapes. For example:
square, triangle, rectangle, pentagon, hexagon

☐ Start the activity:
  ▫ The learners should work together as a whole class or in groups to create a piece of 'modern art' by drawing lines on a piece of paper.
  ▫ They should be able to draw the lines at the same time – they need to sit or stand close together to do this.

☐ They create their piece of modern art.

☐ Ask them to find shapes in the drawing(s). They point them out and discuss them.

☐ If they have worked in small groups, the group which found the largest number of shapes is the winner.

The learners can dictate shapes to each other by describing them. This can be used in a 'content and language integrated learning' (CLIL) lesson for geometry, as it teaches the learners to describe shapes exactly. For extra practice, they could make the shapes three-dimensional.

A further activity would be to give the learners a drawing or a photo, and ask them to pick out the different shapes in it. This could be carried over into a CLIL art class.

Style spectrum

- Describing shapes aloud is auditory.
- Guessing correctly is kinaesthetic emotional.
- Drawing is kinaesthetic motoric.
- Creating a work of art together is global.
- Finding and describing details is analytic.

Putting it together

Strategy
Putting a jigsaw puzzle together to create a picture.

Spotlight on style
Visual

Spotlight on language
Present simple and progressive tense (To practise the present progressive, the picture should have people or animals in it.)

The vocabulary involved is flexible and depends on the picture used – it can be of a classroom, an office, a free-time activity, etc.

--- **Set-up** ---

Make copies of a picture and cut it up as a jigsaw. (This is best done on thicker paper. It should also be coloured paper if the same picture is given to different groups – so you can sort the pieces into packs afterwards.)

--- **Steps** ---

☐ Pre-teach or revise any vocabulary you anticipate as necessary.

☐ Hand out the puzzles for groups or pairs of learners to put together and then talk about the picture:
   ▫ They say what the people are doing – to practise the progressive tense.
   ▫ They talk about items in the picture which are fixed in place – to practise the present simple.

--- ▼ ---

You can prepare *two different* pictures. When the learners have finished putting their pictures together, they work with a new partner who has the other picture and sit back to back. They take turns describing their picture to each other.
▫ The person who is listening can ask questions – but not see the picture.
▫ They then write a description of the picture.
▫ They then describe it to *another* person – who draws it.
▫ The third person then compares their drawing to the original picture.

Style spectrum
- Holding a dialogue is auditory.
- Completing the puzzle is kinaesthetic emotional.
- Moving the pieces around is kinaesthetic motoric.
- Seeing the completed picture is global.
- Describing something exactly is analytic.

I'm looking at something ...

Strategy
Describing where an item in the room is located, so that the others can guess what it is.

Spotlight on style
Visual

Spotlight on language
Spatial pronouns; present simple and progressive tenses

--- **Steps** ---

☐ Pre-teach or revise any vocabulary you anticipate as necessary.

☐ Begin by looking at an item in the room and saying: *I'm looking at something and it is …* (choose a colour).

☐ The learners then ask questions such as:
   ▫ *Is it on the tables?*
   ▫ *Is it near the door?*
   ▫ *Is someone wearing it?*

☐ When someone guesses the item, they are the next one to choose an item for the others to guess.

--- ▼ ---

You can ask the learners to look around the room and then close their eyes. This takes more concentration – as they have to try and fix items in their visual memories rather than just looking for the items.
▫ Choose an item in the room and say: *I'm looking at something* (in a particular part of the room) *and it is* (choose the colour).
▫ The learners ask the same questions as above, but try to remember what they had seen before they closed their eyes.
▫ When someone has guessed correctly, they open their eyes, take another look at the room and then close their eyes again.
▫ The person who has guessed chooses an item – and the procedure is repeated.

Style spectrum
- Asking questions is auditory.
- Guessing the correct answer is kinaesthetic emotional.
- Looking for a physical location is kinaesthetic motoric.
- Observing the classroom as a whole picture is global.
- Using spatial prepositions accurately is analytic.

If I fly to the moon …

Strategy
Describing something belonging to a person
in the room, then guessing the 'trick' behind the game
through observation.

Spotlight on style
Visual

Spotlight on language
Clothing or personal possessions; first conditional

Steps

☐ Pre-teach or revise any vocabulary you anticipate as necessary.

☐ Begin by looking at the person to your right or left and saying:
If I fly to the moon, I will take …

(Mention something the person owns or is wearing – such as a pink jumper, a book bag, etc.)

☐ The learners then begin to make sentences.

☐ Tell them if the objects they mention are things they can take – or not – until they begin to understand the trick.

☐ If one learner has got the idea, ask them if the others can take the items they mention – until everyone has understood how the activity works.

☐ Go round the room until everyone has made a sentence.

▼

Another possibility for practising the first conditional is to begin with the sentence:
If I go to Paris, I will take …
□ The second person says what *they* will take and what *you* will take, and so on, until everyone has repeated the entire list.
□ Ask the learners how they remembered the items – point out that sometimes it is helpful to associate an item with a person when there is a long list to remember.

Style spectrum

- Repeating a grammatical structure aloud is auditory.
- Playing a game is kinaesthetic emotional.
- Thinking about what to take is kinaesthetic motoric.
- Helping others to understand the 'trick' is global.
- Discovering the details of the trick is analytic.

Whose line is the longest?

Strategy
Guessing the length of something by looking.

Spotlight on style
Visual

Spotlight on language
Comparisons

Set-up

You need a tape measure to measure the lines on the board.

Steps

☐ Pre-teach or revise comparatives and superlatives.

☐ Begin by drawing a fairly straight line on the board and marking it with *your* name.

☐ Invite the learners to come and draw lines and mark them with *their* names:
□ The lines can cross each other but must be straight.
□ They can be drawn horizontally, vertically or diagonally.

☐ Put the learners into small groups to discuss the lines and to write down four or five sentences using the following comparative forms:
□ *…'s line is (almost/not) as long as …'s line.*
□ *…'s line is longer/shorter than …'s line.*
□ *…'s line is the longest/shortest.*

☐ The learners read their sentences aloud.

☐ Measure the lines, write the lengths next to them, and ask the learners to tick the correct sentences they wrote.

☐ The group with the most correct sentences is the winner.

The learners can make sentences by looking at each other.
You write them up on the board. For example:
… is the tallest.   *…'s hands are the smallest.*
… is as tall as … .   *… is shorter than … .*
Check the answers by getting everyone to stand up to compare their hands (for example) or supply the correct information.

Style spectrum

- Discussing the length of the lines is auditory.
- Winning the game is kinaesthetic emotional.
- Coming to the board and drawing is kinaesthetic motoric.
- Seeing the overall picture on the board is global.
- Deciding on the length is analytic.

Pass it on!

Strategy
Listening carefully in order to pass on a sentence.

Spotlight on style
Auditory

Spotlight on language
Vocabulary for a specific topic; mixed tenses

Set-up

You will need a whiteboard, chalkboard or flipchart.

Think of an introductory sentence to a lesson – the idea is to introduce a topic and encourage interest in it. The sentence can be on any topic that you plan to teach, but it should be fairly long.

Steps

☐ Divide the class into two groups and whisper your sentence to two learners, one from each group.
   ▫ The learners whisper the sentence to the person next to them – until everyone in their group has heard it.
   ▫ The last person in each group comes to the board – and writes the sentence they heard.

☐ The two sentences are compared. (The final result can be quite funny, depending on how the sentence was changed by the learners.)

☐ The learners make corrections in the written sentences if necessary.

☐ Then they can further discuss what the sentence means – and predict what the lesson will be about.

▼

This activity can also include a 'learner debriefing' which would examine the changes in the sentences. For example:
Did they change anything? What?
Did they try to make the sentence shorter?
Did they simplify words they didn't understand?
Did they try to make 'sense' of the sentence in a different way?

Style spectrum

- Seeing the written version is visual.
- Laughing at the final result is kinaesthetic emotional.
- Sitting close to someone to whisper in their ear is kinaesthetic motoric.
- Working in a large group is global.
- Debriefing is analytic.

Puzzle it out!

Strategy
Putting a riddle in the correct order simply by listening.

Spotlight on style
Auditory

Spotlight on language
Flexible, depending on the riddle, but usually to practise the present or past simple tenses

Set-up

Find a riddle and cut it into strips – each sentence on one strip. There are two riddles opposite, as examples.

Steps

☐ Hand out the strips you have prepared to the learners:
   ▫ They read their sentences aloud.
   ▫ They try to decide on the order of the riddle.

☐ The learners continue reading the sentences aloud in the order they think is correct. They may have to read them several times.

☐ When they have solved the riddle, they explain how they reached the answer.

The learners can be given two different riddles, and have to decide which riddle the sentences apply to:
▫ For advanced groups, this could be done verbally.
▫ For less advanced groups, they would probably need to *see* the strips in order to sort them.

The learners can write out the riddle, making the activity a type of dictation. They can also write out the answers.

A further activity would be to ask the learners to find riddles themselves and bring them to class.

This same technique can be done with scientific processes (the learners then say what the conclusion may be or what type of science it refers to), or with recipes that they put together after hearing the steps (the learners then name the resulting dish), etc.

Style spectrum

- Seeing the strips put together as a story is visual.
- Depending on others in a group is kinaesthetic emotional.
- Holding the strips of paper is kinaesthetic motoric.
- Imagining the story as a whole is global.
- Solving the riddle is analytic.

Puzzle it out!

Mary and the waitress

Mary and the waitress

Mary went into a restaurant and ordered a bowl of soup and a sandwich.

When she finished she asked for the bill, which was eight pounds.

She began counting out the money: 'One, two, three ...', and then said: 'Oh, what time is it?'

The waitress looked at her watch: 'Five, madam,' she said, and Mary continued to count out the pounds: 'Six, seven, eight.'

A young man who was sitting in the corner had been watching all this.

He thought that he could do the same thing.

He came back the next day at lunchtime and ordered a bowl of soup and a sandwich.

When he finished he asked for the bill, which was eight pounds.

He began counting out the money: 'One, two, three ...', and then said: 'Oh, what time is it?'

The waitress looked at her watch: 'One, sir,' and the young man continued to count: 'Two, three, four, five, six, seven, eight.'

How much money did the waitress lose on these two customers?

Answer: She lost nothing.

The glove problem

The glove problem

A woman went into a store to buy a pair of gloves. She chose a pair which cost $8.00.

She paid for them with a $20 bill. The storekeeper had no change because it was very early in the morning.

He asked the woman to wait a moment and went to the restaurant next door.

The owner of the restaurant gave him 20 one-dollar bills for the $20 bill.

The storekeeper returned to his store, gave the woman her change of $12.00 and put the other $8.00 in his cash register.

The woman left the store with the gloves she had bought and her change.

Several hours later, the owner of the restaurant came into the store.

He was very angry and shouted at the storekeeper: 'The $20 bill you gave me was no good! It was counterfeit!'

The storekeeper told the owner of the restaurant that he was very sorry and gave him twenty one-dollar bills.

How much did the storekeeper lose?

Answer: He lost $12.00 and the pair of gloves.

Reconstructing cartoons

Strategy
Describing pictures in a cartoon then putting it in the correct order by listening to the others.

Spotlight on style
Auditory

Spotlight on language
Specific tenses or vocabulary, depending on the cartoon

Set-up

Find a cartoon consisting of at least seven pictures with dialogue and cut it up – each picture on a separate piece of paper. If you have more learners than pictures, they can share one, or you can divide the class into groups.

Steps

☐ Hand out the cartoon pieces you have prepared, one per learner:
- ▫ They describe their pictures and read the dialogue aloud.
- ▫ They work together to decide on the order of the cartoon by listening carefully to each other.

☐ They read aloud the dialogue on the picture again – in the order they think is correct.

☐ Allow them to repeat their information several times, if necessary, in order to get this right.

☐ When they are certain they have the correct order, they describe all the pictures one more time.

☐ Put the cartoon together and let the learners look at it.

☐ To finish off, they can read the lines aloud again after looking at the correct order.

The learners can be given two *different* cartoons and have to decide which cartoon is which.
- ▫ They try to find the people who have pictures from the same cartoon, form groups and put their cartoon together.
- ▫ They describe the finished cartoons to the other groups.

Style spectrum

- Seeing the complete cartoon is visual.
- Laughing together is kinaesthetic emotional.
- Holding the individual pictures is kinaesthetic motoric.
- Creating a whole story is global.
- Ordering is analytic.

Reconstructing texts

Strategy
Putting together texts which have been cut up.

Spotlight on style
Auditory

Spotlight on language
Mixed language, dependent on the text you choose

Set-up

Find an appropriate text and cut it into sections – these cuts should come after *several* sentences, but should be in the *middle* of a sentence.

Steps

☐ Distribute the strips of text to the learners.

☐ The learner with the title and the beginning of the text reads out their information.

☐ They bring the strip of paper to the front of the room and lay it on a desk.

☐ The learner who thinks they have the continuation reads their strip aloud and lays it next to the first one.

☐ The activity continues until the entire text has been reconstructed.

The learners can be asked to do more work with the text:
- ▫ They find alternative ways to continue the text, instead of the original ending.
- ▫ They add adjectives or adverbs to the completed text.
- ▫ They replace words in the text with synonyms.

They can also be asked to write summaries.

Style spectrum

- Looking at the strips of paper with text on them is visual.
- Completing the task is kinaesthetic emotional.
- Getting up to put strips in order is kinaesthetic motoric.
- Creating a complete story is global.
- Constructing the text based on details is analytic.

What's the joke?

Strategy
Listening to the first halves of simple jokes
and matching them to their answers.

Spotlight on style
Auditory

Spotlight on language
Mixed tenses, depending on the joke

Set-up

Find some simple jokes and prepare cards – this will depend
on the number of learners in the class – with the beginning
of the joke on one set of cards and the answers on the other.

The jokes which work best are those with questions and
answers. The ideal is to have one card for each learner – so
that half the class have the question, the other half have the
answer – and they have to find their partners by reading out
their questions and answers.

There are some examples opposite.

Steps

☐ Distribute the cards with the beginnings and the endings:
    ▫ The learners with the *questions* read them aloud.
    ▫ The learners with the *endings* look at their cards and
       decide if they have the appropriate answer.

☐ The activity continues until all the jokes have been
    correctly matched together.

This activity can be used in the formation of pairs of
learners for other activities.

Rather than staying in their seats, the learners can walk
around to find the matching part of the jokes.

Style spectrum

- Seeing the joke is visual.
- Laughing together is kinaesthetic emotional.
- Holding the cards is kinaesthetic motoric.
- Laughing at jokes is global.
- Understanding the point of the joke is analytic.

What is black and white and 'read' all over?	A newspaper.
Waiter, what's this fly doing on my ice-cream?	Skiing, sir.
What did the big chimney say to the little chimney?	You're too young to smoke.
Waiter, what's this fly doing in my soup?	Swimming, sir.
Why are teachers like bank robbers?	They both want everyone to raise their hands.
What do you call a policeman with a banana stuck in each ear?	Anything you like, because he can't hear you.
What runs but never walks?	Water.
What can you make, that can't be seen?	A noise.
What play did the pig read in drama class?	Hamlet.
What subject do sheep study?	Baaology.
Why did the dentist go back to school?	He wanted to brush up on his studies.

Secret identities

Strategy
Guessing the name of a person – in just 20 questions.

Spotlight on style
Auditory

Spotlight on language
Past tense

Set-up

Write out names of famous people from the past on cards. Make sure you choose people your learners would know something about. You will also need some sticky tape (and some blank cards for the alternative suggestion below).

Steps

☐ Fix a card on each learner's back and explain the activity:
  ▫ They are a person from the past, and in order to find out their secret identity they have to ask questions which can be answered with 'Yes', 'No' or 'Maybe'.
  ▫ They move on to another partner after they have asked *two* questions – to ensure they speak to as many people as possible.

☐ You can demonstrate this first:
  ▫ You think of a person who is no longer alive.
  ▫ They ask you questions about the person which can be answered with 'Yes', 'No' or 'Maybe'.
  ▫ They have to guess who the person is.

☐ Start the game.

▼

You can give the learners blank cards and ask *them* to choose the person – this makes the game more personal for them.
▫ You can give them specific categories such as literature, music, sports, art, science, etc.
▫ You may need to assist them in thinking of people, and may want to make sure there are no duplicate names.
▫ They put the name on the back of the person to their right.
▫ Once everyone has guessed, they can talk about the people – and why they chose them.

Style spectrum

- Reading the name of the person is visual.
- Becoming another person is kinaesthetic emotional.
- Moving about is kinaesthetic motoric.
- Guessing who you are is global.
- Remembering details and using them is analytic.

Let me be your guide

Strategy
Describing how a person should move through a maze.

Spotlight on style
Auditory

Spotlight on language
Giving directions; imperatives

Set-up

Create a small maze in the classroom, with chairs and/or desks or other smaller objects. If you can't move furniture easily, you can mark the floor with tape or use objects.

Steps

☐ Pre-teach or revise any vocabulary you think necessary.

☐ Ask for two volunteers:
  ▫ One person will close their eyes and be guided by the other.
  ▫ The 'guide' will tell the 'guided' how to move through the maze.

☐ The 'guide' should use sentences such as:
  ▫ *Take one step to the left.*
  ▫ *Walk two steps straight ahead.*
  ▫ *Turn around.*

☐ Begin the activity.

☐ Finally, ask the learners if it was difficult to concentrate only by listening.

▼

You can put the learners into small groups and tell them to choose a location (or you assign locations that they know).
▫ Tell them they are starting out from the building you are in at the moment.
▫ They have to write instructions for someone who does not know their way around. (You may need to give them vocabulary for giving directions.)
▫ When they have finished, they read out their instructions and the other groups guess where the instructions lead to.

Style spectrum

- Working with a maze is visual.
- Depending on another person is kinaesthetic emotional.
- Moving through a maze is kinaesthetic motoric.
- Observing the social aspect of learner behaviour is global.
- Giving exact instructions is analytic.

Jigsaw listening

Strategy
Completing a text by listening to information.

Spotlight on style
Auditory

Spotlight on language
Mixed language, depending on the topic

Set-up

Prepare a text that practises the grammar, vocabulary or a particular topic you would like to discuss. Write a version for Learner A and a version for Learner B, leaving different gaps (of several words together) in each version. Make copies.

Steps

☐ Put the learners into pairs and give them their texts.

☐ Tell them they have to complete their texts by talking to their partners:
  ◻ They try to find out their missing elements.
  ◻ To do this they can ask their partners questions.

☐ They work together to complete their texts.

☐ Write several comprehension questions on the board, then ask the learners to answer these orally.

☐ Discuss the text and clarify any questions they may have.

You can give half the class *one* text and the other half a *different* text.
◻ Ask them to write a summary of their texts in small groups.
◻ The learners have to find someone who had the other text.
◻ They sit together and listen to the summary. Encourage them to ask questions about it.
◻ The learners who heard the summary then take turns telling the class about the text they heard.
◻ When all the groups have finished, give out the texts the groups did not have, and ask them to read them and compare them with the summaries they wrote.
◻ Discuss any questions which come up.

Style spectrum

- Reading a text is visual.
- Working with a partner is kinaesthetic emotional.
- Writing in the answers is kinaesthetic motoric.
- Helping a partner is global.
- Filling in gaps accurately is analytic.

Emotional objects

Strategy
Finding an emotional connection to an object and discussing its future use, for others to guess what it is.

Spotlight on style
Kinaesthetic emotional

Spotlight on language
The language of emotions; adjectives; *going to* future

Set-up

Bring several objects or photos of objects to class. These can be small soft toys, a special pen or pencil, a CD, a book, a theatre or concert ticket, a train ticket, an apple, etc.

Steps

☐ Put the learners into pairs, or groups of three to five.

☐ Give each pair or group an object or a photo of an object. They should keep it secret.
  ◻ They have to find emotional adjectives *to describe* the object.
  ◻ They then have to decide, as a group, what they are going *to do* with the object in the future.

☐ When they have finished, they say the adjectives out loud and tell the others what they are going to do with the object.

☐ The others have to guess what the object is. Encourage them to use modals by expanding the responses to include '*It could be*' or '*It might be*' when guessing.

The statements could be followed up by asking:
◻ Would the other learners use the same adjectives to describe the object?
◻ Would they use it in the same way?
This can lead to an interesting discussion about perceptions and personal preferences.

The learners can write an emotional description of an object, and ask the others to guess what it could be.

Style spectrum

- Looking at the items is visual.
- Sharing ideas aloud is auditory.
- Handling a photo or object is kinaesthetic motoric.
- Being allowed to choose adjectives is global.
- Finding ways to use something is analytic.

Positive personalities

Strategy
Writing positive adjectives about others.

Spotlight on style
Kinaesthetic emotional

Spotlight on language
Characteristics of personality; adjectives

Set-up

You need to prepare large blank cards with a piece of sticky tape at one end.

Steps

☐ Hand out the cards. The learners put the cards on their neighbours' backs.

☐ They take turns writing *positive* adjectives or personality characteristics on the other learners' cards:
- ▫ They should be encouraged to write *different* words.
- ▫ They shouldn't repeat what others have written.

☐ The learners remove the cards and read what is written.

☐ Others give further examples of the particular characteristic. For example:

| Friendly | *'He was very nice when I began the class and introduced himself right away.'* |
| Helpful | *'When I felt lost she explained things I didn't understand.'* |

The learners can write up descriptions of other learners, using these adjectives, and give examples. The others have to guess who the description is about.

Style spectrum

- Reading the adjectives is visual.
- Listening to the adjectives being read out is auditory.
- Putting cards on someone's back is kinaesthetic motoric.
- Working together as a whole class with one aim is global.
- Choosing appropriate words is analytic.

Horoscope

Strategy
Guessing others' horoscopes, according to descriptions of the signs.

Spotlight on style
Kinaesthetic emotional

Spotlight on language
Adjectives; characteristics of personality

Set-up

Prepare a horoscope which describes personality types. There is an example opposite.

Steps

☐ Ask the learners if they ever look at horoscope pages.

☐ Distribute the horoscope descriptions to the class and make sure that all the vocabulary is clear.

☐ The learners work in pairs or small groups and try to guess which horoscope sign each person is – by looking carefully at the descriptions and pointing out the personality characteristics.

☐ They give their opinions:
- ▫ The people named say if it is true or not.
- ▫ They then tell everyone their horoscope signs.

☐ Each person points out to the class the characteristics in the horoscope which *do* apply to them, and mentions the ones that absolutely *don't* apply.

☐ The class say if they agree or disagree.

The class can write out horoscope descriptions of each other and give reasons for them.

Alternatively, each person can write their *own* horoscope description, which is distributed anonymously so that the other learners have to guess who it belongs to.

Style spectrum

- Reading the horoscope is visual.
- Pointing out words on a page is kinaesthetic motoric.
- Giving opinions verbally is auditory.
- Being aware of personalities is global.
- Reflecting on others is analytic.

Horoscope

⋆ Aries ⋆

The Ram (21 March to 20 April)

They are independent, generous, optimistic, enthusiastic, courageous, and are natural leaders.

They can also be moody, self-involved and impatient.

⋆ Taurus ⋆

The Bull (21 April to 21 May)

They are reliable, loyal, patient, persistent, faithful, and make sure that they finish what they start.

They can also be stubborn, possessive and materialistic.

⋆ Gemini ⋆

The Twins (22 May to 21 June)

They are imaginative, sociable, clever, energetic, talkative, and love freedom.

They can also be superficial, impulsive, restless and indecisive.

⋆ Cancer ⋆

The Crab (22 June to 22 July)

They are loyal, caring, loving, sympathetic, dependable, and act according to their feelings.

They can also be moody, self-pitying and oversensitive.

⋆ Leo ⋆

The Lion (23 July to 21 August)

They are ambitious, generous, loyal, confident, motivated and inspiring to others.

They can also be stubborn, melodramatic and vain.

⋆ Virgo ⋆

The Young Girl (22 August to 23 September)

They are observant, dependable, helpful, charitable, faithful, and do things carefully to make sure they are perfect.

They can also be fussy, interfering and sceptical.

⋆ Libra ⋆

The Scales (24 September to 23 October)

They are diplomatic, peaceful, hospitable, idealistic, communicative, and like to be around other people.

They can also be superficial, indecisive and unreliable.

⋆ Scorpio ⋆

The Scorpion (24 October to 22 November)

They are passionate, resourceful, loyal, dynamic, secretive, and like to be in control.

They can also be jealous, unyielding and manipulative.

⋆ Sagittarius ⋆

The Archer (23 November to 22 December)

They are independent, optimistic, adventurous, honest, outgoing, and like exploring new places and ideas.

They can also be reckless, direct and intolerant.

⋆ Capricorn ⋆

The Sea-goat (23 December to 20 January)

They are practical, responsible, resourceful, loyal, ambitious, and like to work quietly and effectively.

They can also be dictatorial, inhibited and suspicious.

⋆ Aquarius ⋆

The Water-carrier (21 January to 19 February)

They are witty, inventive, clever, original, intellectual, and take pride in being unique.

They can also be stubborn, unemotional and sarcastic.

⋆ Pisces ⋆

The Fishes (20 February to 20 March)

They are accepting, imaginative, compassionate, adaptable, idealistic, and find value in helping others.

They can also be oversensitive, self-pitying and indecisive.

Sources:

http://zodiac-signs-astrology.com
http://www.astrology.com.au/astrology/12-signs-of-the-zodiac/

It's in the cards

Strategy
Telling each other's fortunes.

Spotlight on style
Kinaesthetic emotional

Spotlight on language
Future tenses

Set-up

Bring fortune-telling cards to class. These can often be found in stationery shops. They generally include words such as 'treasure', 'stranger', etc. Alternatively, you can use the samples opposite.

Steps

☐ Put the class into pairs.

☐ Each learner chooses four or five cards, which they give to their partner.

☐ The partner then creates a story about what will happen in the future to the person whose cards they are 'reading'.

The class can make their own fortune-telling cards. You will need to provide the learners with any necessary vocabulary:

☐ You can write words like the following on the board (or give out a list):

castle	*gold ring*
money	*bad luck*
stranger	*good luck*
love	*four-leaf clover*
marriage	*hidden treasure*

☐ Alternatively, you can start by brainstorming words with the class – ask them what might come up in a fortune-telling session and write up on the board the words they call out.

Give the learners time to make the cards – they should write the word and draw a picture on the card. The procedure is then the same as described above.

cloud	key	castle
tall, dark stranger	young man	young woman
old man	old woman	money
cat	dog	small house
lake	bridge	tall building
airplane	boat	four-leaf clover
sun	moon	stars
face with big smile	mountain	snow
hidden treasure	love	gold ring

Style spectrum

- Using cards or drawing pictures to make cards is visual.
- Telling a story is auditory.
- Manipulating cards is kinaesthetic motoric.
- Putting a story together is global.
- Arranging a logical order is analytic.

Planning a trip

Strategy
Planning an excursion together.

Spotlight on style
Kinaesthetic emotional

Spotlight on language
Linking words; first conditional; *going to* future

Set-up

Prepare cards with an amount of money written on them. The amounts can vary, but there should be enough for a group to plan activities for an evening, a weekend or a longer trip. (This will have to be decided *before* you prepare the cards with money.)

Steps

☐ Put the learners into groups and ask each group to take a card.

☐ Tell them that this is how much money they have to plan an evening, a weekend or a longer trip together (whichever you decided):
  ▫ They write out what they are going to do.
  ▫ They have to make sure that activities are included for *each person* in the group.

☐ They then read their plan to the others – and discuss.

▼

The learners write up a journal report after the trip – imagining what happened and how things went.

Outlines

Strategy
Tracing each other on large pieces of paper.

Spotlight on style
Kinaesthetic emotional

Spotlight on language
Parts of the body; adjectives

Set-up

Bring to class large pieces of paper and things to draw with (pens, pencils, crayons, highlighters). If the pieces of paper are not large enough, you may have to tape them together.

Steps

☐ Place the pieces of paper on the floor and hand out the drawing equipment.

☐ The learners take turns lying down on the pieces of paper and tracing each other's bodies.

☐ They then write positive adjectives in different areas of the drawing to express how they feel about each other.

☐ They present each other to the class, and explain why they have written what they have.

▼

The learners can write up a description of another learner at home, using positive adjectives. This can then be used as the basis for:
- an essay about another person
- a description of a good friend
- an 'opinion piece' on what characteristics they look for in friends, colleagues, partners, etc
- a character reference for a job

Style spectrum

- Writing a journal report is visual.
- Planning aloud is auditory.
- Talking about activities is kinaesthetic motoric.
- Planning a trip together is global.
- Staying within a budget is analytic.

Style spectrum

- Looking at the shape of the bodies is visual.
- Explaining is auditory.
- Lying on the floor is kinaesthetic motoric.
- Drawing people is global.
- Finding details about others is analytic.

Roll a mood

Strategy
Using a dice to start a conversation about emotions.

Spotlight on style
Kinaesthetic emotional

Spotlight on language
Emotions and feelings; linking words; mixed tenses

Set-up

You need to bring a dice to class.

Steps

☐ Elicit different emotions or feelings, and assign one to each number on the dice (eg 1 = *happy*, 2 = *excited*, etc).

☐ Put the learners into groups.
  ▫ They roll the dice.
  ▫ They make sentences according to the emotion or feeling, corresponding to the number.

For example:
I feel happy when/because …
I feel sad so I am going to …
When I feel upset I …
The last time I was excited was when …
If I get angry, I will …

The learners can brainstorm emotions and feelings, and their cause and effect. For example:
I feel happy when …
When … happens, I feel sad.
Hearing about … makes me glad.
I saw a … and as a result I am …
They then use this language to write a story explaining a strong emotion or feeling they have had.

These can be shared with the class or, if they prefer, just given to the teacher.

Style spectrum

- Looking at the numbers on the dice is visual.
- Listening to the others is auditory.
- Rolling the dice is kinaesthetic motoric.
- Being creative, based on the number rolled, is global.
- Constructing 'cause and effect' sentences is analytic.

It makes me feel …

Strategy
Talking about pictures or photos and the effect they have on the learners.

Spotlight on style
Kinaesthetic emotional

Spotlight on language
Emotions; adjectives; linking words

Set-up

Find photos or drawings, reproductions of artwork, etc, and bring them to class.

Steps

☐ The learners choose a drawing or photo and talk about how it makes them feel:
  ▫ They give reasons for their feelings.
  ▫ They explain exactly *what* in the picture evokes that particular emotion.

☐ More advanced classes can elaborate on various aspects of the drawing:
  ▫ dark or light colours, subdued or bright colours
  ▫ actions or people in the drawing or photograph
  ▫ style of the artist or photographer
  ▫ landscapes or skies
  ▫ number of people or objects in the drawing or photo
  ▫ the sounds they imagine
  ▫ what they think will happen next, and why, or what they think happened just before the photo was taken

You can pin up photos or drawings around the room and the learners walk around and choose one:
  ▫ They write about the emotions it evokes.
  ▫ They read out what they have written, and the others guess which photo or drawing it refers to:
  This photo makes me feel … because …
  When I look at this photo I feel …

Style spectrum

- Observing a picture is visual.
- Describing a picture is auditory.
- Picking up a picture is kinaesthetic motoric.
- Considering a picture as a whole is global.
- Describing a picture in detail is analytic.

It's in the bag

Strategy
Trying to guess items of vocabulary which the learners can feel but cannot see, to raise curiosity about a particular subject.

Spotlight on style
Kinaesthetic motoric

Spotlight on language
Vocabulary for a specific topic; mixed tenses

Set-up

Bring to class a number of small items in a closed plastic bag. Try to have approximately as many items as learners. For example:

- ☐ For a general English class: small objects such as a pen, paper clip, marker, etc
- ☐ For a business English class: office supplies, etc
- ☐ For a class of engineers: small technical items, etc

Steps

- ☐ Pass the bag you have brought around the room:
    - ☐ Each learner feels one item in the bag.
    - ☐ They try to guess what it is.

- ☐ Continue passing the bag around until each of the learners has had a chance to touch an item and make a guess.

- ☐ Take the items out one by one, and show them to the class.

- ☐ Go over the names of the items, and write them up on the board if necessary.

The learners can be asked to describe what the items feel like by using adjectives, or to imagine what the purpose of the items could be. This language can be exploited at the end – when the learners have seen what is in the bag.

They could also make suggestions for additional items, or categorise the ones which have been presented to them.

Style spectrum

- Seeing the items afterwards is visual.
- Discussing the objects and their use is auditory.
- Finding if guesses are correct is kinaesthetic emotional.
- Touching and imagining what the things are is global.
- Stating what things are used for is analytic.

Creating a machine

Strategy
Becoming a machine.

Spotlight on style
Kinaesthetic motoric

Spotlight on language
Processes; movements; parts of machines; sequencing words; mixed tenses

Steps

- ☐ Put the learners into groups.

- ☐ Tell them to think of a fun machine with different parts which it would be useful to have. Examples could be:
    - ☐ a 'baby bathing' machine
    - ☐ a 'washing, drying, putting away dishes' machine
    - ☐ a 'noodle-making, cooking and serving' machine
    - ☐ a 'getting someone dressed' machine

- ☐ Encourage the learners to be as creative as possible:
    - ☐ They decide which *person* can play which *part* of the machine.
    - ☐ They decide which *order* the process should occur in.

- ☐ They demonstrate how the machine works for the other groups, who try to guess what the function of the machine is.

- ☐ One of the learners can act as a moderator and explain what each part of the machine is doing.

- ☐ When they have finished, the learners explain what they have produced.

This activity can then be followed up for homework, in which they write out the process.

More advanced groups can put the entire process into the passive voice.

Style spectrum

- Watching the others act out their machines is visual.
- Discussing the machine is auditory.
- Creating a machine together is kinaesthetic emotional.
- Imagining an entire process is global.
- Ordering the steps is analytic.

Back-writing telephone

Strategy
Passing on a word from one learner to another.

Spotlight on style
Kinaesthetic motoric

Spotlight on language
Mixed vocabulary, chosen by the learners

Steps

☐ The learners stand in a line, one in front of the other, facing forward – in groups of at least six.

☐ The learner at the back of the line thinks of a word:
  ◦ They 'write' it on the back of the person in front of them.
  ◦ This can be repeated as often as necessary, until the person feels that they know what the word is.

☐ The person who has just 'received' the word then writes it on the back on the person in front of them, who passes it on until it has reached the first person in the line.

☐ The first person then goes to the back of the line and writes it on the back of the person who started the word.

☐ The group then says what word they think it is.

☐ If necessary, you can write the word up on the board.

▼

The learners could try not just words, but collocations or short sentences.

Another variation would require more concentration – as several words are passed along:

◦ The learners stand in a circle of five to eight people. Each receives a different short word from the teacher.
◦ The words are passed on, as before, except that the learners are continually receiving and then passing new words on round the circle.
◦ The game ends when the words come back to those who first wrote them.

You can also stop the game if you want to check which word the learners think has just been written on their back.

Style spectrum

- Seeing the word on the board at the end is visual.
- Hearing the word said aloud is auditory.
- Touching another person is kinaesthetic emotional.
- Understanding a word as a 'whole' is global.
- Deciphering the individual letters is analytic.

Mime artist

Strategy
Acting out verbs or processes for others to guess.

Spotlight on style
Kinaesthetic motoric

Spotlight on language
Action verbs; present progressive tense

Set-up

You will need one blank card for each learner.

Steps

☐ Give each learner a blank card and ask them to write an action verb or a particular process on the card:
  ◦ It could be a simple one like washing and drying dishes.
  ◦ It could be one with more steps – like changing a tyre on a car or bicycle.

☐ The cards are then re-distributed randomly to other learners:
  ◦ With action verbs, they can act out individually what is on the card.
  ◦ With processes, this could be done in pairs – with two people acting it out.

☐ The others have to guess what the action verb or the process is.

▼

The learners can write the processes out for homework. Remind them to use sequencing words to make the processes clear.

More advanced classes can put the processes into the passive voice.

Style spectrum

- Watching the others mime is visual.
- Talking about the words is auditory.
- Roleplaying is kinaesthetic emotional.
- Working on a common outcome is global.
- Ordering steps is analytic.

Acting out adverbs

Strategy
Miming actions.

Spotlight on style
Kinaesthetic motoric

Spotlight on language
Verbs; adverbs

Set-up

Prepare two sets of cards, one with *verbs* and one with *adverbs* or *adverbial expressions*. See the examples opposite. Pre-teach the vocabulary and explain how adverbs are created if necessary.

Steps

☐ Put the sets of cards in two piles in front of the class.

☐ One learner picks a card from the 'verb' pile and a card from the 'adverb' pile.
  ☐ The learner acts out the two words.
  ☐ The others guess *what* the learner is doing and *how* they are doing it.

☐ The person who has guessed correctly chooses the next two cards.

▼

Several learners can be sent out of the room while the class chooses an adverb.
☐ They come back in.
☐ Volunteers carry out actions – demonstrating that adverb.
☐ The learners who were out of the room have to guess which adverb they are using.

A further variation would be for the learners to draw stick figures on cards – doing an activity which the others act out.

Another variation is for them to mime their actions and adverbs to a partner, who then mimes them to the class – without knowing what the words are – for them to guess.

(I got the original ideas for this activity from Penny Ur, and have adapted and extended them.)

Style spectrum

- Observing the others mime activities is visual.
- Expressing oneself verbally is auditory.
- Having fun is kinaesthetic emotional.
- Guessing the words is global.
- Analysing the movements is analytic.

The actions

take a shower	wash the dishes
dance a waltz	park the car
climb a tree	work on the computer
brush your teeth	drive a car
eat spaghetti	drink coffee
make a cup of tea	cross a busy street
read the newspaper	correct papers
ride a bike	take off your jacket

The adverbials

carefully	carelessly
politely	impolitely
loudly	quietly
excitedly	calmly
happily	sadly
sleepily	energetically
in a concentrated way	absent-mindedly
in a friendly way	in an unfriendly way

Sticky-note body

Strategy
Naming and labelling parts of the body.

Spotlight on style
Kinaesthetic motoric

Spotlight on language
Parts of the body

Set-up

You need to bring tape or sticky labels to class.

Steps

☐ Revise names for parts of the body if you think necessary.

☐ Being by asking if two learners would volunteer to have sticky labels or tape attached to them in an activity and don't mind being touched by others.

☐ Make sure that is this agreed and acceptable to the learners you have – teenagers, mixed groups, etc.

☐ Divide the class into two groups, with one volunteer in each group.

☐ Both groups are given labels and a time limit:
　□ They have to write as many words for body parts as they can think of on the labels.
　□ They will then attach them to the volunteer.

☐ When you say 'Stop', they take the labels off and count how many different words they have written.

☐ The group who has written the most is the winner.

The learners can go on to practise the words:
□ They try to remember which ones they stuck on first or removed first.
□ One learner in the group can be appointed the 'scribe' – writing down all the words as the others say them.

(I learned this game from Petra Preede.)

Style spectrum
- Writing the words is visual.
- Talking about the words is auditory.
- Letting others get close to you is kinaesthetic emotional.
- Working as a team is global.
- Organising the activity is analytic.

This is my knee

Strategy
Naming parts of the body in a 'concentration and practice' activity.

Spotlight on style
Kinaesthetic motoric

Spotlight on language
Parts of the body

Steps

☐ Begin the activity by saying:
This is my knee.
As you do it, point to a *different* part of your body (such as your head).

☐ Tell the class that the next person has to point to the part of their body that you *said*, not the one you *pointed to*, but that they have to *say* a *different* part of the body.

☐ Explain that it is natural to say a word and point to the object with that name – but that the 'trick' of this game is to listen and then react kinaesthetically by doing something else.

☐ The first learner points to their head and says:
This is my stomach.

☐ The game continues in this way, with the next learner pointing to the part of the body that was named (in this case: 'stomach') – but saying a *different* part.

☐ The game finishes when each learner has said something and pointed to something:
　□ It winds up back at the teacher who points to the part that the last learner said.
　□ The teacher could end it by pointing and saying the *correct* word.

You can give the learners a drawing of a person and ask them to label the different parts. This can be done in groups, with the groups competing against each other to write as many words as possible within a time limit.

Style spectrum
- Watching the others is visual.
- Listening carefully is auditory.
- Playing a game together is kinaesthetic emotional.
- Having fun is global.
- Concentrating on being accurate is analytic.

Becoming a statue

Strategy
Making a statue.

Spotlight on style
Kinaesthetic motoric

Spotlight on language
Parts of the body; sequencing words; past tense

Steps

☐ Ask one learner to come to the front of the class and stand as if they were a statue.

☐ Invite another learner to join them and become part of the statue.

☐ One by one, invite a number of learners to become *more* parts of the statue.

☐ As the learners join in, they should be encouraged to change something in the statue so that a completely new picture is made each time.

☐ When the statue is complete, the learners sit down.

☐ Ask what happened.

☐ The learners explain the process in the past tense. (This makes the past tense real for them, as the teacher can point out that the statue is no longer there so it is a completely finished action.)

▼

Depending on the class, this can be a fun photo opportunity.

The learners can write out what happened. Encourage them to use sequencing words and describe the situation exactly, using the past tense.

Style spectrum

- Looking at the statue being built is visual.
- Discussing the steps is auditory.
- Being close to others is kinaesthetic emotional.
- Creating a unified entity is global.
- Remembering the sequence is analytic.

Becoming a picture

Strategy
Explaining a picture to others, who try to 'become' the picture.

Spotlight on style
Mixed VAK

Spotlight on language
Spatial prepositions; imperatives; present progressive and present simple

Set-up

Find a photo which has several people doing something.

Steps

☐ Tell the learners you need volunteers to 'be a picture'. The number of volunteers will depend on the number of people in your picture.

☐ The picture is then passed around the class:
  □ Make sure the volunteers can't see it.
  □ Each learner takes a turn to tell the volunteers what they need to do.
  □ Subsequent learners can make corrections to the picture, as it is passed around.

☐ When the class is satisfied, the volunteers are allowed to see the picture.

Before the volunteers see the picture, they can try to guess what the situation is:
  □ They can use the past or the present perfect tense to explain what has led up to the situation.
  □ They can use the future to say what they think will happen next.
This can be expanded when they see the original picture.

The learners can write a story based on the picture, using *before*, *during* and *after*.

Style spectrum

- Describing a picture is visual.
- Listening carefully is auditory.
- Volunteering to work in a group is kinaesthetic emotional.
- Posing as a character is kinaesthetic motoric.
- Working together is global.
- Describing details is analytic.

Back-to-back drawing

Strategy
Describing a picture to each other.

Spotlight on style
Mixed VAK

Spotlight on language
Spatial prepositions; present progressive and simple tenses

Set-up

Find a simple drawing you can show on an OHP, or with presentation software. Alternatively, you can make copies for the learners.

Steps

☐ Tell the learners to sit back to back, with one learner as the 'explainer' and the other as the 'artist'.
  ▫ The explainer *will* be able see the image.
  ▫ The artist will *not*.

☐ Turn on the OHP, or give half the learners your pictures:
  ▫ The learners who are explaining see the picture and begin to describe it.
  ▫ The others draw the picture.

☐ The *artists* may ask as many questions as they like; however, the *explainers* must not see what they are drawing.

☐ When they have finished, they can look at the original.

The learners can sit back to back and create their own drawings which they describe to their partners. Their partners draw them and then compare the finished products. This works well with drawing furnishings and rooms.

A second variation is to send one learner out of the room:
▫ Show the others a drawing which they have to remember.
▫ Call the learner back in, and ask the others to explain the drawing to the learner – who draws it on the board. The others are allowed to see and correct the drawing.
▫ Finally, you show the original to the 'artist'.

Style spectrum

- Picturing something in your mind is visual.
- Hearing instructions is auditory.
- Sitting close to your partner is kinaesthetic emotional.
- Drawing is kinaesthetic motoric.
- Depending on your partner is global.
- Asking for details is analytic.

Memory

Strategy
A card-matching game.

Spotlight on style
Mixed VAK

Spotlight on language
Mixed vocabulary, according to the topics you want to practise

---

Set-up

Find 'words + pictures', 'words + collocations' or 'words + translations/definitions', depending on what you want to practise and the level of your class. Put the words, phrases, pictures, etc, on one side of a card. Leave the other side blank.

Steps

☐ The learners are put into groups and each group is given a set of cards, turned face down:
  ▫ They have to match the words and translations/definitions, etc, together by turning over two cards at a time and saying the words on the cards aloud.
  ▫ They take turns and, when they find a pair, they say the word(s) aloud and have another go. If the cards don't match, the next person continues.

☐ The person with the largest number of pairs is the winner.

This activity can also be used to practise phrases which go together (eg *How are you? – Fine, thanks.*) or situations and phrases which go together. For example:
You accept an offer for help:
Thank you. That would be very nice.
You ask someone for their opinion:
What do you think about …?

Alternatively, the learners can make their own cards with the vocabulary they want to practise. This can be done in different groups and when they have finished preparing their cards, they pass their words to another group to play the game.

Style spectrum

- Remembering the location of something is visual.
- Saying words aloud is auditory.
- Playing in a group is kinaesthetic emotional.
- Turning cards over is kinaesthetic motoric.
- Seeing the whole picture is global.
- Remembering specifics is analytic.

VAK bingo

Strategy
Playing bingo by turning cards over.

Spotlight on style
Mixed VAK

Spotlight on language
Mixed vocabulary – according to what you want to practise.

Set-up

Make cards with pictures of specific vocabulary on them. Each learner should have the same number of cards (five or six). These can be pictures of food, parts of the body, furniture, areas in a town, symbols, actions, etc).

Steps

☐ Distribute the cards you have prepared.

☐ The learners lay the cards in front of them, face up.

☐ Call out the names of the items and, if a learner has the item, they turn the card over, putting it face down.

☐ The first person to turn over all their cards is the winner.

☐ The learners turn their cards face up again.

☐ They must then name each of the cards that have been turned over – saying the name and seeing the picture.

This activity can also be used with phrases. For example, where particular prepositions are missing:

☐ You read out the prepositions.
☐ The learners turn their cards over if they have sentences where these prepositions are used.

Style spectrum

- Looking at words or pictures is visual.
- Hearing words called out is auditory.
- Trying to win a game is kinaesthetic emotional.
- Turning cards over is kinaesthetic motoric.
- Learning vocabulary in a game is global.
- Concentrating on details is analytic.

Your last holiday

Strategy
Guessing holiday places.

Spotlight on style
Mixed VAK

Spotlight on language
Free-time activities; holiday words; past tense

Set-up

Find photos of holiday places and bring them to class.

Steps

☐ Choose a photo and get the learners to ask you 'yes/no' questions about the holiday. For example:
Did you fly there?
Was the trip longer/shorter than …?

☐ When a learner has guessed the place, give them one of the photos. The others have to ask questions about it.

☐ Encourage them to ask detailed questions in order to find out as much as possible before guessing. For example:
Did you understand the language that was spoken there?
Were there special things to eat or drink?
Was there traditional entertainment?
Did you do indoor or outdoor activities?
Was the weather pleasant?

☐ Once they have guessed correctly, let the class see the picture. (The learners do a lot of guessing and have to make use of a wide range of vocabulary, and then enjoy looking at the holiday pictures at the end of the activity.)

The learners can write a story about their last holiday without mentioning where they were. They read the stories aloud and the others have to guess where they went.

The learners can write postcards to the class from the places in the game. These can also be written without mentioning the name of the place so that the others have to guess.

Style spectrum

- Looking at the photos at the end of the activity is visual.
- Responding to questions is auditory.
- Imagining being on holiday is kinaesthetic emotional.
- Handling photos is kinaesthetic motoric.
- Imagining a range of activities is global.
- Thinking of questions is analytic.

Look: no mistakes!

Strategy
Filling gaps with words or phrases on cards.

Spotlight on style
Mixed VAK

Spotlight on language
Mixed language, depending on the text you choose

Set-up

Prepare a gapped text and put the missing words on cards, rather than on the page that has the text.

Steps

☐ Put the learners into groups and give them the text and a set of cards.

☐ They need to find the correct words to put into the gaps.

☐ Encourage the groups to lay the cards out on their desks and agree the correct order *before* they write the words into the text.

☐ Check the order of the words and make sure that they have the correct order so that they can complete the text correctly and not have to cross out mistakes.

▼

The gaps can be of prepositions in set phrases, or they can be collocations which need to be put together first before they fit into the gaps.

Alternatively, collocations can be put together as dominoes – so that when the learners have found the correct collocation for a gap, they have the first part of the collocation for the next gap. This variation is presented in detail – in a business English context – in *In Business* (Cambridge Copy Collection – CUP 2005).

This activity works well for songs with gapped texts.

Style spectrum

- Choosing words on cards and reading a text is visual.
- Discussing answers is auditory.
- Coming to an agreement is kinaesthetic emotional.
- Laying out cards is kinaesthetic motoric.
- Completing the text together is global.
- Logically choosing the correct answer is analytic.

Interesting definitions

Strategy
Repeating and remembering definitions.

Spotlight on style
Mixed VAK

Spotlight on language
Unusual vocabulary

Set-up

Find unusual words and their definitions and write them on cards. You will need at least one card per learner. There are some examples opposite.

Steps

☐ Give out the cards, one to each learner:
   ▫ The learners read their card
   ▫ They try to remember the definition.

☐ They then walk around the classroom and explain to the others the word they were given.

☐ Each learner repeats what they last heard to the next person.

☐ When you stop the game, the learners say the last word they heard and what they remembered about the definition.

☐ The learner who had the original definition reads it aloud.

▼

This activity can be used to introduce new or specific vocabulary.

It can be done using a 'snowball' technique – the cards are passed from one learner to another, ensuring that each learner reads and says the definition.

Another variation would be for the *learners* to find new words and their definitions and bring them to class. These could then be practised in the same way.

Style spectrum

- Reading the definitions is visual.
- Passing on the information is auditory.
- Working with others is kinaesthetic emotional.
- Walking about is kinaesthetic motoric.
- Learning unusual or funny words is global.
- Passing on exact information is analytic.

Interesting definitions

kenspeckle (adj)
easily recognisable or distinguishable, something that is conspicuous

amphigory (n)
a poem designed to look good but which does not make sense

mumpsimus (n)
A wrongly-held opinion; or a person who believes something incorrectly

famulus (n)
a private servant or secretary, especially to a magician or scholar

growlery (n)
a place to go and think when you are in a bad mood

orphrey (n)
gold thread used to embroider clothing, especially clothes worn by clergy

tintinnabulate (v)
to ring like a bell, the word describes the sound bells make

withershins (adv)
counterclockwise or in a contrary direction

phrontistery (n)
an establishment for study and learning

farrago (n)
a confused mass of objects or people or any disordered mixture

galimatias (n)
nonsense, a confused mixture of unrelated things

mascaron (n)
a grotesque face on a door knocker

barathrum (n)
a person who is insatiable

carfax (n)
a place where four roads come together and form a junction

pilgarlik (n)
a poor wretch; used in a self-pitying way to refer to oneself

ultracrepidate (v)
to criticise beyond the sphere of one's own knowledge

villipend (v)
to make light of, to disparage mockingly

xenium (n)
a gift made to an ambassador or guest, any compulsory gift

jeremiad (n)
a lamentation or prolonged complaint, an angry or cautionary harangue

liripipe (n)
the long tail of a graduate's hood or a lesson committed to memory

nepenthe (n)
a drink or drug that makes one forget suffering

quincunks (n)
an arrangement of five items, four in the corners of a square and one in the middle

enchiridion (n)
a book carried in the hand for reference, especially one used for music or theology

selcouth (adj)
strange, unfamiliar and marvellous, combining strangeness with a sense of wonder

spatchcock (v)
to insert into a text inappropriately or hurriedly; origin: stuffing and cooking a bird immediately after killing it

tregetour (n)
a juggler, trickster or deceiver, someone who uses cunning tricks to deceive another person

miasma (n)
foul vapours emitted from rotting matter, unwholesome air or atmosphere

Source:
http://phrontistery.info/favourite.html

Who went where?

Strategy
Asking questions about creative excursions.

Spotlight on style
Mixed VAK

Spotlight on language
Travel words; past tense

Set-up

You need blank cards with sticky tape at one end for each learner.

Steps

☐ Write the following on the board:
Where?	*Accommodation?*
When?	*Means of transport?*
Who with?	*Purpose?*
For how long?	*Surprise?*

☐ Give out the cards and ask the learners to write the answers to the questions on the cards in a few words (eg *Where?* – the moon; *Surprise?* – took wrong suitcase). They should be as creative as possible (they can include trips to the moon, honeymoons, etc).

☐ Collect the cards and put them on the back of another learner. That learner must walk around, asking the others the questions to get the answers on their back. These would include: *Where did I go? Who did I go with?* etc.
  ▫ They should get no more than two answers from each of the others.
  ▫ They should note down the answers.

☐ When they have got all the information, they look at their cards and tell the stories of their trips to the class.

The learners can write out their trips as homework.

(This idea was adapted from a game by Ernst Korper.)

Style spectrum

- Writing information on a card is visual.
- Asking questions and responding to them is auditory.
- Imagining a creative holiday is kinaesthetic emotional.
- Moving from person to person is kinaesthetic motoric.
- Finding out about the holiday is global.
- Noting down answers is analytic.

Run and dictate

Strategy
Writing down a text dictated by another learner.

Spotlight on style
Mixed VAK

Spotlight on language
Mixed

Set-up

Pin texts up on the walls of the room. These can be the same text, different texts or parts belonging to one text.

Steps

☐ The learners work in pairs or groups:
  ▫ One learner is the 'runner'.
  ▫ The runner goes to the text, comes back and repeats as much as they remember.
  ▫ The partners write it down.

☐ Then the runners return to the text and tell their partners the next part.

☐ When they have finished, they compare their texts with the text on the wall.

If you chose different parts of one text, the learners have to put it together at the end. This should be done orally, with each group reading their part aloud.

The groups can appoint a new runner after several sentences, so that different learners move about:
▫ The person who is the new runner hands their text over to the person who had been the runner.
▫ This person now continues to write the text.

This activity can be done in a 'round robin' by constantly changing the runners. The texts should finally be checked for spelling and accuracy.

Style spectrum

- Remembering written texts is visual.
- Dictating is auditory.
- Helping a partner is kinaesthetic emotional.
- Running is kinaesthetic motoric.
- Remembering a text as a whole is global.
- Remembering individual words is analytic.

Run and draw

Strategy
Explaining and drawing simple figures in a grid.

Spotlight on style
Mixed

Spotlight on language
Shapes; spatial prepositions

Set-up

Prepare a grid with simple figures drawn in some of the squares. For large classes, have several copies. Prepare a blank one for the learners.

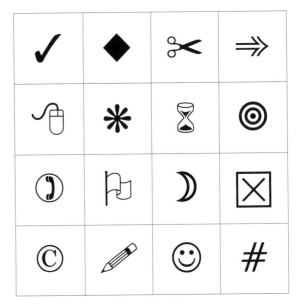

Steps

☐ Pin the grid with the figures on the wall and give the learners each a blank grid.

☐ The learners will work in pairs:
  ▫ One person is the 'runner'.
  ▫ The other person will have to reconstruct the grid.

☐ Begin the activity:
  ▫ The runner should not be allowed to see what their partner is doing.
  ▫ The runner goes to the grid and reports what they see.
  ▫ The other person draws the figure in the correct box.

☐ When they have finished, they compare with the original.

▼

This can be done with *words* or *sentences* in the grid, instead of drawings.

The grid could have more boxes for more advanced groups.

If the learners are working independently in pairs, they each need a different grid, with different symbols, and each learner needs a blank one.

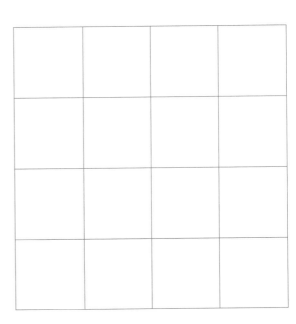

It could also be done as a back-to-back activity. They should not see the other person's grid and must listen carefully, but they *can* ask questions to clarify things.

Style spectrum

- Looking at symbols or pictures is visual.
- Describing what you have seen is auditory.
- Collaborating with a partner is kinaesthetic emotional.
- Moving quickly from place to place is kinaesthetic motoric.
- Remembering a complete grid is global.
- Remembering the positions of symbols is analytic.

Chapter Three

Global–Analytic learning styles

The Global–Analytic cognitive processing chapter is dedicated primarily
to activities aimed at global or analytic learners, but also includes
a number of activities which would appeal to both styles.

A fuller explanation of how the content of the activities
has been structured is presented on page 28.

Global

- Write a story
- Complete the conditionals
- What would you do …?
- Circle faces
- Listen and change
- Buzz words
- You–Robot

Analytic

- The 'yes-no' hotseat
- Do you want to bet?
- Mark the map
- Detective story
- Logic puzzle
- What are the rules?
- Five in a row
- Ask the right question

Mixed Global–Analytic

- Initial adjectives
- Animal, vegetable, mineral
- Coded interviews
- Roll an answer
- Word hunt
- It's on the box
- The envelope game

Write a story

Strategy
To work as a group and write a story
about another group.

Spotlight on style
Global

Spotlight on language
Everyday activities; past tenses or future tenses

Steps

☐ Divide the class into groups of three or four.

☐ Tell each group which of the other groups they have to write about.

☐ Give them a time frame for a story. For example:

What did the other group do last weekend?
What is the group going to do next weekend?

☐ Give them 10–15 minutes to write a story including each person in the group.
  - ◻ They should invent activities that the people did together, or are going to do together.
  - ◻ They should discuss among themselves and decide what types of activities the other group might have done together, or might do together, by observing them.

☐ Go round and monitor, offering help if necessary.

☐ Ask the learners to read out their stories.

▼

The learners can be asked to write out the stories again at home:
- ◻ They hand them in as homework.
- ◻ Alternatively, they send you the stories digitally – you make whatever corrections are necessary and return them to the class.
This can become part of a class portfolio.

Style spectrum

- Organising a logical story is analytic.
- Observing others is visual.
- Discussing ideas is auditory.
- Inventing information about others is kinaesthetic.

Complete the conditionals

Strategy
To write one half of a sentence, which will then
be matched randomly with a second half.

Spotlight on style
Global

Spotlight on language
Conditional sentences

Set-up

Decide before you begin if you want to practise the first, second or third conditional.

You will need strips of paper in two different colours, one colour for each half of the class.

Steps

☐ Pre-teach or revise conditional sentences, if necessary – according to the tense you want to focus on.

☐ Give half the class one coloured strip of paper and the other half the different colour.

☐ Put the learners into pairs with different colours and tell them that they are each going to write one clause of a conditional sentence:
  - ◻ They decide who is going to write the 'if' clause and who the 'result' clause.
  - ◻ These will be on the different coloured strips of paper.

☐ They write their clauses, using the pronoun *we*.

☐ When they have finished, collect the strips of paper.

☐ Volunteer learners take any two strips (one of each colour) and read the completed sentence aloud until all of them have been read: Which sentences were the best, funniest, most interesting, most possible, etc?

In pairs, the learners can write out a number of stem sentences in the conditional you want to practise. These are given to another pair, who complete the sentences. The first pair then choose several to read aloud.

Style spectrum

- Using the correct form of a tense is analytic.
- Reading sentences is visual.
- Listening to completed sentences is auditory.
- Creating sentences together is kinaesthetic.

What would you do ...?

Strategy
To work as a class and come up with ideas of what to do in hypothetical situations.

Spotlight on style
Global

Spotlight on language
Second conditional sentences

Steps

☐ Send two people out of the room.

☐ Tell the rest of the class that a particular situation has occurred and they have to think of ideas of what they would do in this situation. For example:

It rained ice cream.

☐ Encourage the learners to try and give interesting, humorous and creative answers.

☐ Call the two people back to the room and tell them they have to ask everyone in the room this question:

What would you do if this happened to you?

☐ Each person in the class must answer the question using the form:

If this happened to me, I would …

☐ When everyone has answered, the two learners posing the question can try to guess what the situation was.

☐ If they cannot guess, they can go on by asking:

What else would you do if this happened to you?

☐ They keep asking questions until they are able to guess the situations.

▼

The learners can choose the funniest, best, most interesting answers – and write out the sentences again for homework.

They can also think of more situations themselves for a future class.

Style spectrum

- Guessing an answer based on clues is analytic.
- Imagining a situation is visual.
- Listening to responses is auditory.
- Finding humorous answers is kinaesthetic.

Circle faces

Strategy
To draw a face collaboratively and create a story about it.

Spotlight on style
Global

Spotlight on language
Personal appearance and personality characteristics; hobbies; family/work-related vocabulary

Set-up

You need one piece of blank paper and coloured pens for each pair of learners.

Steps

☐ Put the learners into pairs and give each pair a blank sheet of paper and some coloured (felt-tip) pens.

☐ Tell the learners they are going to draw parts of faces, according to the instructions you will be giving them:
   □ Each group will begin by drawing a circle on their papers which fills about three-quarters of the page.
   □ Each time they have finished drawing the facial feature you mention, they have to pass their papers to their neighbours on the right.

☐ The learners draw, in turn and according to your instructions: a nose, eyes, mouth, ears, hair, other features they feel are missing (jewellery, freckles, etc).

☐ Tell them they now have a picture of their 'new friend'. They should work together in pairs and decide:
   □ How, where and when did they meet?
   □ What is the person's name? What do they do?
   □ Do they have a family? What are their hobbies?
   □ What activities do they do together?

☐ The pairs then introduce their friends to the class, and answer any questions the other learners might have.

The learners can write a short story about their new friend, including the information above, as homework.

Style spectrum

- Deciding on facts is analytic.
- Drawing a face is visual.
- Creating a story with others is auditory.
- Imagining information is kinaesthetic.

Listen and change

Strategy
To tell stories to each other, change them
and pass them on.

Spotlight on style
Global

Spotlight on language
Everyday activities; past tenses

Set-up

You will need small strips of paper.

Steps

- ☐ Give each learner in the class a small strip of paper and instruct them to write their name on it.

- ☐ Tell them to think of some small problem they had in the last week. Stress that these problems should be minor ones – give them an example:
  I forgot to buy milk for my coffee so had to drink tea.
  - ◻ In pairs, they tell each other their 'stories'.
  - ◻ They exchange the strips of paper with their names.

- ☐ Explain that they are going to tell the story they heard to another person – but should slightly change some details. They will also exchange the strip with the name.

- ☐ The activity continues until the learners have heard and passed on at least five or six stories. Remind them not to tell a story to the person who it originally belonged to.

- ☐ Stop them – they tell the last story they just heard.

- ☐ The people listening guess if it is *their* story and, once they have guessed correctly, they tell the class the original.

The learners can write out the final stories they heard at home and hand them in. Alternatively, you get them to send you the stories digitally: you make any necessary corrections and return them to the learners to be part of a class portfolio.

(I learned this activity in a workshop with Andrew Wright and have adapted it slightly.)

Style spectrum

- Remembering details is analytic.
- Seeing the names on cards is visual.
- Exchanging stories orally is auditory.
- Mingling is kinaesthetic.

Buzz words

Strategy
To choose a group of words and then use them
to put a story together.

Spotlight on style
Global

Spotlight on language
Mixed vocabulary; mixed tenses

Steps

- ☐ Divide the class into groups of three or four.

- ☐ Tell each group to quickly brainstorm and write down about 20 words – these can be of their own choosing or you can give each group a topic.

- ☐ Give them 10–15 minutes to write a story incorporating each of their words. It is important that the words are used *logically* and that *correct tenses* are used for the verbs.

- ☐ Go round, monitoring and offering help if necessary.

- ☐ The groups then read their stories aloud.

- ☐ The class listen to all the stories and decide:
  - ◻ Which was the most original?
  - ◻ Which was the most interesting?
  - ◻ Which was the most creative?
  - ◻ Which was the funniest?

The learners can write out the stories for homework. They can then send them digitally – so that they can be used in a class portfolio and distributed to the others.

Once they have been written out, they can be used again in class with comprehension questions, or for discussions of particular topics.

Style spectrum

- Using all the words in a logical manner is analytic.
- Writing words or stories is visual.
- Brainstorming is auditory.
- Working in a group is kinaesthetic.

You–Robot

Strategy
To give instructions in order to get each other to carry out actions.

Spotlight on style
Global

Spotlight on language
Imperatives; present progressive tense

Steps

☐ Put the learners into groups of three or four. Pair each of these groups with a second group.

☐ Explain that one group of learners are 'programmers' and the others are 'robots'.
  □ The programmers will tell the robots what to do.
  □ The robots will follow the instructions.

☐ Explain the procedure:
  □ The instructions should include the *exact* actions the robots make.
    For example: *pick something up, move something*, etc.
  □ These movements should all be part of a single process:
    For example – washing the dishes:
    Pick up a dish. / Turn on the water. / Hold the dish under the water. / Take a sponge and wash the dish. / Rinse off the soap. / Put the dish in a dish rack.

☐ Then they change places – the *new* programmers now tell the *new* robots what to do.

☐ Each 'robot' then performs their movements in front of the class. The learners who were not the programmers for these particular robots have to guess what the process is that the robot is carrying out.

▼

The learners think of something they would like a robot to perform for them. For example: *drive them home from class* or *iron their clothes*. They write out their movements exactly.

Alternatively, they can make simple stick drawings that show exactly what the robot needs to do. They then give these pictures – in the correct order – to their robots to act out.

Style spectrum

- Putting a sequence together is analytic.
- Watching someone move is visual.
- Listening to instructions is auditory.
- Carrying out a movement is kinaesthetic.

The 'yes-no' hotseat

Strategy
To work together as a class to guess what one learner is thinking about by asking questions.

Spotlight on style
Analytic

Spotlight on language
Questions; modals of possibility; mixed tenses

Set-up

It might be necessary to prepare cards with famous people or activities to give the learners, instead of asking them to think of something themselves.

Steps

☐ Brainstorm possible ways to answer questions, including those using modals, and write the answers on the board.

☐ Ask a volunteer to come to the front of the class and sit in the 'hotseat'.
  □ Tell the volunteer to think about a famous person or an activity they themselves like to do.
  □ Tell the rest of the class that they can ask the person questions to try and guess what or who they are thinking about.

☐ The person cannot answer *yes* or *no*. If they say *yes* or *no*, they go back to their seats and another person takes their place.

☐ When a learner guesses the person or activity, they come to the front of the room and are the next person to occupy the 'hotseat'.

▼

The learners can write mini-dialogues in which nothing is answered with *yes* or *no*. For example: *Would you like some coffee? – Maybe later, thanks.*

This activity can also be done by answering every question with a question. For example:
How old are you? – How old do you think I am?
Are you tired? – Why, do I look tired?

Style spectrum

- Playing a game is global.
- Looking at the others is visual.
- Responding is auditory.
- Sitting in the 'hotseat' is kinaesthetic.

Do you want to bet?

Strategy
To work with a partner to find mistakes in a text.

Spotlight on style
Analytic

Spotlight on language
Phrasal verbs, dependent prepositions; mixed tenses, modals

Set-up

Create a text with mistakes. This can be done by using examples that the learners have written and compiling a list with the most common mistakes. See below for some examples of mistakes and the instructions for the activity.

Steps

- ☐ Give each learner a copy of your list and explain the instructions.
- ☐ Tell them to follow the instructions in pairs.
- ☐ When they have finished, go over the answers in open class.

- ☐ Award the points.
- ☐ Ask the learners *why* particular words were wrong. For example:
  - ▢ preposition missing in phrasal verb
  - ▢ wrong tense
  - ▢ verb not agreeing with noun

▼

The learners can write the text out correctly at home.

They can also be asked to keep a list of common mistakes to use in their future writing endeavours. See *The perfect page* on page 88.

Sentence	Correction	Points bet	Points won	Points lost	Total
1 I slept long this morning.					
2 Can you borrow me your pencil?					
3 What means this word?					
4 I am here since January.					
5 Went he home early?					
6 If I would see her, I would tell her.					
7 I am going to my class every day.					
8 He remembers me of my brother.					
9 I am interesting in that film.					
10 I have known him since many years.					
				GRAND TOTAL:	

Instructions

Work with a partner and look at the sentences.

Find the mistakes and correct them.

You can bet 10, 20, 30, 40 or 50 points that your corrections are the right ones:
- If you are right, you will be awarded the points you bet.
- If you are wrong, you will lose them.

Start correcting!

Style spectrum

- Checking a text for errors is analytic.
- Reading a text is visual.
- Deliberating aloud is auditory.
- Circling, underlining or crossing out words is kinaesthetic.

Mark the map

Strategy
To work out where shops and other facilities in a town are located, by looking at a map and reading clues.

Spotlight on style
Analytic

Spotlight on language
Public buildings/shops; spatial prepositions

Set-up

Copy one map for each group of learners. Also copy the cards opposite and cut them up, one set for each group.

Steps

☐ Tell the class that some money is hidden somewhere in a town.

☐ Divide the class into small groups, and give each group a map and a set of clue cards.

☐ Tell the groups to work together:
  ▫ They have to figure out where the shops and public buildings are located.
  ▫ They read the clues to each other, which will lead them to a finished map through a process of elimination.

☐ Now tell the learners the final clue:
  The money is in the north-east corner of the courtyard with the shops where people can buy a sofa for their home or ingredients for preparing a meal.

☐ Finally, you can hand out the Key, and discuss how difficult it was to complete the map.

▼

The learners can write out instructions to get from a starting point to another place in town. They can use the map provided – or a real map from their own city.

They practise all the words used for giving directions. They can also do this in the form of a dialogue, and should be encouraged to ask questions so that they demonstrate they understood the directions correctly.

Style spectrum

- Collaborating is global.
- Finding places on the map is visual.
- Listening to the clues is auditory.
- Working with manipulatives (maps and cards with clues) is kinaesthetic.

Clue cards

The shoe shop is across the street from the library.	The bank is next to the town hall.
The camera shop is on the northeast corner.	The souvenir shop is across the street from the flower shop.
The bookshop is between the antiques shop and the shoe shop.	The jewellery shop is next to the clothing shop.
The food shop is on the southeast corner.	The café is next to the library.
The bakery is next to the antiques shop.	The clothing shop is across the street from the mobile phone shop.
The vegetarian restaurant is next to the post office.	The restaurant is not far from the antiques shop.
The young fashions shop is next to the outdoor market.	The electronics shop is next to the clothing shop.
The mobile phone shop is next to the magazine stand.	The cinema is between the restaurant and the bus terminal.
The butcher's is on the northwest corner.	The gift shop is between the electronics shop and the camera shop.
The home furnishings shop is across the street from the town hall.	The stationery shop is next to the young fashions shop.

Mark the map

Map

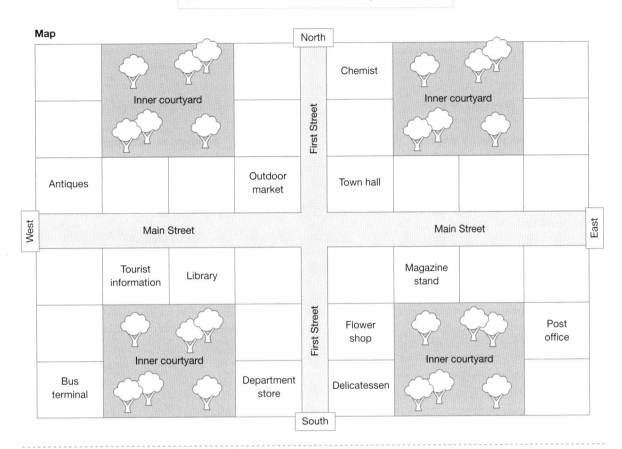

Key

Butcher's			Stationery shop		Chemist			Camera shop
Bakery			Young fashions	First Street	Bank			Gift shop
Antiques	Bookshop	Shoe shop	Outdoor market		Town hall	Jewellery store	Clothing shop	Electronics store
Main Street					Main Street			
Restaurant	Tourist information	Library	Café		Home furnishings	Magazine stand	Mobile phone shop	Vegetarian restaurant
Cinema			Souvenir shop	First Street	Flower shop			Post office
Bus terminal			Department store		Delicatessen			Food shop

Detective story

Strategy
To work together as a group, to come up with a plausible story about an event that happened.

Spotlight on style
Analytic

Spotlight on language
Places; events; past tenses

Set-up

Collect authentic materials such as flight, train or bus tickets, theatre tickets, restaurant business cards, maps, etc, as clues.

Steps

☐ Divide the class into groups of three or four and give out some of the clues to each of the groups.

☐ Tell the learners that a man has disappeared and the police are trying to figure out:
  □ where he had been
  □ what he had been doing before this happened

The clues were found in the last place he was seen.

☐ The group uses the clues to put together the story of the past 24–48 hours.

☐ Tell the learners that they have to use each of the clues and give a logical explanation of why they were found in this place.

☐ When they have finished, they read their stories aloud.

▼

According to the level, you can tell the learners that each group had only a part of the clues and they now have to work as a whole class to put the entire story together.
□ You help them with the vocabulary they need.
□ You help them to create the final story.

They can write it up for homework and include it in a class portfolio.

Style spectrum

- Constructing an entire story is global.
- Looking at the authentic materials is visual.
- Deliberating aloud in a group is auditory.
- Arranging the clues is kinaesthetic.

Logic puzzle

Strategy
To solve a problem in a text, through reading clues and a process of elimination.

Spotlight on style
Analytic

Spotlight on language
Mixed

Set-up

Copy the grid and the clues opposite.

Steps

☐ Put the class into pairs and give each pair a grid and the clues (these can all be on separate pieces of paper instead of on one sheet).

☐ Tell each pair that they need to solve the puzzle, and give them a time limit (10 minutes should be enough).

☐ Check the answers in open class and ask the learners to explain how they decided on their answers.

▼

The learners can be asked to write out logic puzzles like these for the others and bring them to class. You would need to correct them first, however, but this type of activity encourages logical thinking.

Another type of text which can be used can be found in the 'Auditory' section of Chapter Two (*Mary and the waitress* and *The glove problem*) on page 45.

Style spectrum

- Coming to a logical conclusion is analytic.
- Looking at clues is visual.
- Deconstructing the clues is auditory.
- Getting strips of paper to read clues from is kinaesthetic.

Logic puzzle

Who stayed in which room?

Read the clues and figure out:

- Who stayed in which room?
- What type of room did the people have?
- How long did they stay?
- Which meals did they have at the hotel?

	101	102	201	202	203
Name					
Type of room					
How long					
Meals taken					

1 Room 101 is below Room 201, and 102 is below 202.

2 Jane Smith was in room 102.

3 The man who had full board had a room on the ground floor.

4 The woman on the ground floor stayed for three nights.

5 One room on the first floor is a double room and the room below it is also a double room.

6 The woman who stayed for a week was in room 202.

7 Two brothers stayed in single rooms on the first floor and only had breakfast. They both stayed for the same number of nights.

8 The woman on the first floor only had breakfast.

9 The man who was next to Jane Smith had a single room for four nights.

10 The person who stayed in the double room on the first floor is named Carolyn Jones.

11 One person had breakfast and dinner at the hotel.

12 Bill Winter does not have a brother who stayed at the hotel.

13 John McCoy stayed in the room above Bill Winter for two nights and has a brother named Jack.

Key				
101 Bill Winter single 4 nights full board	102 Jane Smith double 3 nights breakfast dinner	201 John McCoy single 2 nights breakfast	202 Carolyn Jones double a week breakfast	203 Jack McCoy single 2 nights breakfast

Adapted from *Friends 4 – Activity Book* Veritas Verlag 2006

What are the rules?

Strategy
To put together rules for a specific situation,
using modal verbs.

Spotlight on style
Analytic

Spotlight on language
Modals; imperatives

Steps

☐ Review modal verbs if necessary – ensure that the class understand the differences between *must*, *do not have to*, *must not*, *should*, *can*, etc.

☐ Ask the learners to make up rules for the *classroom*.

☐ Elicit them and write them on the board.

☐ Now brainstorm *different* situations with the learners. For example:
  ◻ being a successful language learner
  ◻ riding a bike in the city
  ◻ being a customer in a shop
  ◻ eating pizza in a restaurant

☐ Try to find at least 10–12 situations, encouraging the class to be as creative as possible.

☐ Put the learners into small groups:
  ◻ They have to choose one of the situations you have brainstormed.
  ◻ They have to write between six and eight rules for these situations.

☐ Go round and monitor if necessary.

☐ When they have finished, they read out their rules for the others to guess which situation the rules refer to.

You can ask the learners to look on the internet for unusual rules in different cities or countries.
◻ They choose their favourite one and bring it to class.
◻ They read it aloud.
◻ The others guess where the rules are from.

Style spectrum

- Making up creative rules is global.
- Writing down rules is visual.
- Reading the rules aloud is auditory.
- Working in groups is kinaesthetic.

Five in a row

Strategy
To create questions which fit short answers,
based on the roll of a dice.

Spotlight on style
Analytic

Spotlight on language
Question forms

Set-up

Copy the board opposite for each learner and provide one dice for each pair of learners.

Steps

☐ Put the learners into pairs and distribute the dice and the boards.
  ◻ One learner will be 'X'.
  ◻ One learner will be 'O'.

☐ Explain that the aim of the game is to get 'five in a row'.

☐ The learners take turns:
  ◻ They decide who is X and who is O.
  ◻ They take turns rolling the dice.
  ◻ The person who rolled the dice chooses a number in the boxes at the bottom of the board that correspond to the number rolled on the dice.
  ◻ They have to make a question which logically fits the short answer given.

☐ Once a learner has made a question which both agree is correct, the learner who chose the square marks it with their X or O.
  ◻ That square has been taken.
  ◻ It cannot be used by the other member of the pair.

☐ The game ends when one of the learners has 'five in a row': horizontally, vertically or diagonally.

☐ If the learners finish before all the squares have been used, they can work together to make questions to fit the other phrases.

Style spectrum

- Making creative questions is global.
- Choosing squares to get 'five in a row' is visual.
- Asking questions is auditory.
- Rolling a dice is kinaesthetic.

Five in a row

1 From the vending machine.	**2** It's five pm.	**3** You can take the bus.	**4** At the newsstand.	**5** At 8 am.	**6** Fine, thanks.
7 For the last six years.	**8** In 2010.	**9** Last March.	**10** About three weeks.	**11** Not very often.	**12** Mostly in the evenings.
13 Not more than 80 kph.	**14** Every month.	**15** Spaghetti and fish.	**16** A boss.	**17** Every morning.	**18** Almost never.
19 In front of the building.	**20** Across the street.	**21** In the country.	**22** In Europe.	**23** About 350.	**24** Four to five hours a day.
25 Our English teacher.	**26** Tenses.	**27** Films.	**28** Everything except sports.	**29** Yesterday.	**30** Because it's necessary.
31 Over and over.	**32** Next week.	**33** Prepositions.	**34** My friends.	**35** On Saturday.	**36** At home.

1	**2**	**3**	**4**	**5**	**6**
3, 7, 16, 24, 26, 35	1, 9, 18, 21, 29, 31	5, 10, 14, 19, 30, 33	6, 11, 13, 23, 28, 36	2, 8, 15, 22, 25, 32	4, 12, 17, 20, 27, 24

▼

The learners can work in groups of three or four, and think of different short responses. They read these out to the others who have to think of appropriate questions. Encourage the others to think of as many questions as possible to fit an answer. For example:

'More than 500' could have questions like:
- □ *How many friends do you have on Facebook?*
- □ *How many books do you have at home?*
- □ *How many books have you read?*
- □ *How many songs are on your mp3 player?*

Ask the right question

Strategy
To choose words from a text (or any material you have worked on) and ask questions to get each other to say them.

Spotlight on style
Analytic

Spotlight on language
Mixed language, depending on the words the learners choose

Steps

- ☐ Put the learners into pairs and ask them to look through a text or other class material:
  - ▫ They should choose ten words they would like to review, and write them down.
  - ▫ They should think of questions they can use which would be answered by the words they have chosen.

- ☐ Put the pairs together with another pair, and tell them they have five minutes to get their partner to say their words.

- ☐ Stop them after five minutes, and tell them to switch roles and try to guess the other's words.

- ☐ When they have finished, ask them to discuss any words which were not guessed.

The learners can use their list of words to make word fields or find the opposites of the words they have chosen:
- ▫ They can then write gap sentences for the others to fill in.
- ▫ This can be used to build vocabulary and review classwork.

Style spectrum

- Playing a guessing game is global.
- Looking through a text or class material is visual.
- Listening to questions is auditory.
- Collaborating with a partner is kinaesthetic.

Initial adjectives

Strategy
To find adjectives which start with the first letter of the learners' first names and which describe them.

Spotlight on style
Global–Analytic

Spotlight on language
Adjectives

Steps

- ☐ Ask the learners to think of an adjective which starts with the same letter as their first name.

- ☐ They go around the room and introduce themselves. For example:

  I am wonderful Wendy.

- ☐ They are not allowed to choose the same adjective as another person:
  - ▫ If a learner cannot think of one, the class can help.
  - ▫ Alternatively, they can use a dictionary to find an adjective.

- ☐ When the class have all chosen their adjectives, go around the room and see how many of the adjectives the others can remember.

- ☐ This can be repeated in the next lesson, and can be a helpful way to remember names at the beginning of a course.

You can use the adjectives to make up stories about the learners. Put them into groups:
- ▫ They write a short story about themselves.
- ▫ They find examples of why the adjectives they chose suit them.
- ▫ They read the story aloud for the others.
- ▫ The others give their opinions or ask questions.

Doing this as homework could provide another element for a class portfolio.

Style spectrum

- Finding unusual adjectives is global.
- Finding accurate adjectives is analytic.
- Working with letters is visual.
- Remembering the adjectives you heard is auditory.
- Associating a person with an adjective is kinaesthetic.

Animal, vegetable, mineral

Strategy
To work in open class to guess which item
another learner has described.

Spotlight on style
Global–Analytic

Spotlight on language
Adjectives which describe products

Set-up

Find pictures of everyday items from adverts. Cut them out
and mount them on card.

You might find it helpful to prepare, and possibly pre-teach,
a range of useful adjectives, such as the ones opposite.

battery-operated	large	technical
beautiful	light	translucent
comfortable	luxurious	transparent
electrical	mechanical	ugly
electronic	metallic	uncomfortable
expensive	necessary	unnecessary
fragile	portable	unusual
fun	practical	useful
hard	rectangular	user-friendly
heavy	round	usual
impractical	soft	washable
inexpensive	square	waterproof
inflatable	sturdy	water-resistant

Steps

☐ Explain that everything is made of animal, vegetable or
mineral elements. Give examples:
    ▫ leather or wool (animal)
    ▫ paper or wood (vegetable)
    ▫ plastic or glass (mineral)

☐ Demonstrate first – you can use an everyday item such as
a ladder.
    ▫ Explain that it can be vegetable (wooden) or
      mineral (aluminium); is rectangular or triangular (a
      stepladder); is sturdy, practical and can be light-weight
      and portable.
    ▫ The learners then ask questions and you answer with
      'Yes', 'No' or 'Maybe'.

☐ Give one learner the picture of an item and ask them to
say if it is animal, vegetable or mineral and then use four
or five adjectives to describe it.
    ▫ The others ask questions using other adjectives – until
      someone guesses what the item is.
    ▫ You can limit the number of questions to 20.

☐ The learner who guesses correctly then gets a picture and
follows the procedure above.

The learners can write an advert for a product and bring it
to class:
▫ They read their advert aloud or pass it around.
▫ The others have to guess what product is being described.

This game is also available electronically and can be found
as an app for several brands of smartphones, although in the
electronic version the questions include not only adjectives
but also uses, etc.

Style spectrum

- Playing a game is global.
- Thinking of the specifics of items is analytic.
- Looking at pictures is visual.
- Asking and answering questions is auditory.
- Touching the pictures is kinaesthetic.

Coded interviews

Strategy
To get personal information and remember it by using symbols or drawings.

Spotlight on style
Global–Analytic

Spotlight on language
Personal information

Set-up

You will need small pieces of paper.

Steps

☐ Give out your slips of paper.

☐ Tell the learners that they are going to interview three people in the class and get specific information about them. This can include:
- where they are from
- what they do
- the hobbies they have
- what they are good or bad at doing

☐ When the interviewee answers, the interviewer makes a note on their piece of paper using a small drawing or symbol to remember what the answer was.

☐ When everyone has interviewed three people, ask the learners to choose one of the people and introduce them to the class, using what they noted down.

☐ Make sure that everyone is introduced.

▼

The learners can be allocated one of the people in the class and asked to conduct a longer interview:
- They can then write these up as a homework assignment.
- The interviews can be corrected and added to a class portfolio.

(I learned this activity from Petra Preede.)

Style spectrum

- Finding out personal information from others is global.
- Assigning abstract symbols to facts is analytic.
- Drawing or using symbols is visual.
- Interviewing is auditory.
- Moving about is kinaesthetic.

Roll an answer

Strategy
To give opinions or reasons for something.

Spotlight on style
Global–Analytic

Spotlight on language
Words of cause and effect; expressing opinions

Set-up

You need dice. If you have a large 'styrofoam' one, this works very well as you can roll it on the floor. If not, give out a few dice so that each learner can reach one easily.

Steps

☐ Choose a topic or activity that your learners know something about. Roll a dice and explain:
- An *odd* number means they have to express that number of *negative* aspects of the topic. For example: a 3 means giving three reasons they don't like something, or three reasons against doing something.
- An *even* number means they have to express *positive* views on the topic. For example: a 2 means giving two reasons for doing something, or two arguments in favour of the topic.

☐ Begin the game – the learners may not repeat what another learner has said.

☐ The topic is changed when the learners can't think of anything more to say on a particular topic.

The topics can be chosen by the class. For example: '*A class excursion to a museum*' or general topics in the news.

The learners can choose one or two of the topics discussed and write down the arguments they heard in *favour* or *against*. This is excellent training for essay writing where the learners need to look at both sides of a topic and express them:
- They write their essay, using these different arguments.
- They finally give their own opinion of the topic.

Style spectrum

- Basing arguments on the roll of a dice is global.
- Finding arguments is analytic.
- Looking at the numbers on the dice is visual.
- Listening to and remembering what others say is auditory.
- Rolling the dice is kinaesthetic.

Word hunt

Strategy

To remember words a partner has said.

Spotlight on style

Global–Analytic

Spotlight on language

Personal characteristics; words for emotions

| Set-up |

Make a copy of the board opposite for each learner and prepare some small pieces of paper (for covering the words).

| Steps |

☐ Hand all the learners the boards and the pieces of paper.

☐ Clarify any words they don't know.

☐ Get the learners to sit across from each other in pairs in such a way that they can't see their partner's board:
   ☐ Learner A says a word – and covers it on their board.
   ☐ Learner B then says a different word – and covers it.

☐ They continue choosing words randomly until one learner says a word that their partner has already said – at which point, the game ends.

☐ They do the activity again – it will be more challenging the *second* time because they may remember words they heard the *first* time – and therefore make a mistake.

☐ When they have finished, ask them to discuss any strategies they used to remember the words their partners said.

▼

The learners can choose several of the words and use them to describe people they know. They should give specific examples as to why they assigned these characteristics or emotions to these people.

This step can also be done as homework – the learners write about the characteristics that are important to them in their friends.

(This game was designed by Dr Gudrun Zebisch.)

Style spectrum
- Concentrating on emotions is global.
- Finding strategies is analytic.
- Remembering the placement of words is visual.
- Saying words aloud is auditory.
- Covering the words with paper is kinaesthetic.

generous	affectionate	capable
happy	carefree	humorous
empathetic	creative	brave
innovative	eager	energetic
optimistic	enthusiastic	sensible
flexible	helpful	well-balanced
cheerful	friendly	imaginative
calm	organised	sensitive
joyful	open-minded	direct
lively	sociable	loving
hard-working	decisive	spontaneous
natural	persistent	well-informed
fair	determined	self-confident
positive	reliable	punctual

It's on the box

Strategy
To work together as a group to solve a jigsaw puzzle and then write questions about it.

Spotlight on style
Global–Analytic

Spotlight on language
Advertising language; food ingredients

Set-up

Cut up several cereal boxes (or other authentic food packages) into pieces like a jigsaw puzzle.

Steps

☐ Divide the class into groups of three or four.

☐ Give each group one of the puzzles. (This works best if you put each puzzle into an envelope and label it with the name of the cereal, for example.)

☐ Tell each group to put the puzzle together:
  ▫ When they have finished, they write five or six questions based on the information found on the boxes. This can be about the marketing techniques, the nutritional information or the ingredients, etc.
  ▫ When they have finished, they leave their puzzle and the questions, and move clockwise to the next group, where they read the questions and write their answers.
  ▫ When they have finished, they move clockwise again, checking the answers to the questions written by another group and making corrections, if they wish.

☐ The learners then go back to their original cereal box – the questions and answers – and check if the other learners answered their questions correctly.

The learners can then have a discussion in open class about the food products they have looked at. They can talk about the marketing techniques, the nutritional value of the ingredients of the products – and compare them.

Style spectrum

- Putting a jigsaw puzzle together is global.
- Writing detailed questions is analytic.
- Looking for information on the boxes is visual.
- Expressing opinions in class is auditory.
- Moving pieces around to make a puzzle is kinaesthetic.

The envelope game

Strategy
To decide which job would be perfect for each other.

Spotlight on style
Global–Analytic

Spotlight on language
The language of jobs

Set-up

You need envelopes and lots of slips of paper for each learner.

Steps

☐ Brainstorm jobs that the learners know or have heard of:
  ▫ Get as many jobs as possible written up on the board.
  ▫ Encourage the learners to come up with unusual jobs.

☐ Distribute the envelopes and the pieces of paper and ask the learners to write their names on the envelope.

☐ They pass the envelope to the person on their right:
  ▫ That person thinks about the ideal job for this person.
  ▫ They write it on a piece of paper.
  ▫ They put it into the envelope and pass it on.

☐ The next person decides which job would be good for the person on the envelope and writes the job on a piece of paper, adding it to the first job – without looking inside.

☐ Continue until the envelopes return to their owners.

☐ The owners of the envelopes then open them and look at the suggested jobs. They categorise them into groups:
  ▫ Jobs they would like to have.
  ▫ Jobs they might like to try.
  ▫ Jobs they would never want to do.

☐ The learners all tell the class which jobs were suggested for them, and which ones they would or wouldn't like.

☐ They can ask for the reasons for their suggestions.

The learners can write a short essay on their ideal job: Why would they like it? Why would they be good at it?

Style spectrum

- Finding out which jobs were chosen for you is global.
- Deciding on a job for someone is analytic.
- Writing the jobs is visual.
- Telling the others about the suggested jobs is auditory.
- Filling and passing on the envelopes is kinaesthetic.

Chapter Four

Mind Organisation learning styles

The Mind Organisation chapter concentrates on four distinct behavioural styles. Activities are first presented for each of these learner types, and a final section contains activities which stretch over more than one style.

A fuller explanation of how the content of the activities has been structured is presented on page 28.

Flexible Friend

- Personal goals
- Emotional dictation
- Deep impact
- All about my partner
- Personal mindmaps
- What we have in common

Expert Investigator

- The perfect page
- Just give me the facts
- Nothing but the facts
- Internet investigation
- Researching an excursion

Power Planner

- How does it work?
- Is everything in order?
- Group grammar
- Confirming information
- Setting priorities
- Linking ideas

Radical Reformer

- Radical roleplay
- Act out the characters
- Can you sell it?
- The restaurant game
- When I was a child …
- Our ideal home

Mixed Mind Organisation

- The department store
- Our type of trip
- Don't say the word!
- My first time …
- Your last chance

Personal goals

Strategy
The learners fill in a questionnaire about their goals for a course. They compare these at the end of the course to see which were reached.

Spotlight on style
Flexible Friend

Spotlight on language
Likes and dislikes; goals; future tenses

Set-up

Make copies of the 'Your personal goals' questionnaire opposite for all the learners.

Steps

- ☐ Hand out the questionnaire.
- ☐ The learners fill it out individually.
- ☐ Volunteers comment on what they wrote.
- ☐ The finished questionnaires go into their personal folders.

▼

The class can come up with their *own* personal questionnaire by brainstorming ideas, which you write up on the board. The learners then fill it out individually – as above.

The class are then asked to keep learner diaries throughout the course, which they can share with you if they wish. At the end of the course, they reflect on their goals, as above, and draw conclusions as to how well they reached their goals or the methods they used.

Style spectrum

- Drawing conclusions is enjoyed by Expert Investigators.
- Designing a questionnaire is enjoyed by Power Planners.
- Finding creative answers is something enjoyed by Radical Reformers.

Your personal goals

Think about your goals in taking this course and answer the questions below. Find creative answers if possible.

1 What do you hope to learn regarding the language?

- A What vocabulary do you specifically want to learn?
- B What areas of grammar do you feel you need to practise?
- C Do you want to become a more confident speaker? In which situations?
- D Do you want to be able to take part in discussions more easily?
- E Is it important for you to learn to write more cohesively or better stylistically? Why?
- F Do you need to read with better understanding? Which types of texts?
- G Do you want to understand spoken speech better? In which situations?
- H Do you want to improve your general communication skills and make yourself understood?

2 What do you hope to take away from the course regarding personal relationships?

- A Make new friends.
- B Get to know colleagues better.
- C Networking opportunities.

3 What else do you hope to learn or experience?

- A Information about different cultures and traditions.
- B Understand how others think and what is important to them.
- C Enjoy yourself and have fun.
- D Be intellectually challenged.
- E Anything else?

Emotional dictation

Strategy
The learners practise listening strategies
and write down sentences which apply to *them*.

Spotlight on style
Flexible Friend

Spotlight on language
Likes and dislikes; facts and feelings;
personality characteristics; mixed tenses

Set-up

Use the sentences supplied opposite, or make up your own –
their complexity will depend on the level of the class.

Steps

☐ Read out your sentences.

☐ The learners write the ones which apply to them:
  ☐ They exchange their papers with a partner.
  ☐ They talk about the sentences and compare them.
  ☐ They find out what they have in common.

▼

The learners can be given copies of the sentences – to check
they wrote everything down correctly. They proceed as
follows:
☐ They make mindmaps based on their answers.
☐ They write up stories about their partner.
☐ They report to another person about their partner's
  sentences.
☐ They organise the sentences into categories.

If the class would like to know specific information about
each other, they can call out their *own* sentences (which
relate to them personally) for you to write down. You then
choose randomly from these for your dictation.

The class can add these statements to a language portfolio or
to their language folders.

They can expand them into a personal story about
themselves which could be used as a homework assignment.

(I learned this idea in a workshop with Sheelagh Deller.)

- I am single.
- I am married.
- I have a child/children.
- I am in a relationship.
- I live in the city.
- I live in the country.
- I work in an office.
- I have been to London.
- I like doing sports.
- I enjoy relaxing with a book.
- I enjoy chatting with other people.
- I am very outgoing.
- I am often shy in groups.
- I like to tell jokes.
- I have never written a letter to a newspaper.
- I have a pet.
- I would love to travel around the world.
- My dream is to write a novel.
- I would like to try an extreme sport like bungee-jumping.
- My friends are people who I can laugh with.
- I was drinking coffee or tea ten minutes ago.

Style spectrum

- Listening carefully and analysing statements is enjoyed
  by Expert Investigators.
- Organising sentences is enjoyed by Power Planners.
- Having lots of options is enjoyed by Radical Reformers.

Deep impact

Strategy
The learners express their feelings about a story.

Spotlight on style
Flexible Friend

Spotlight on language
Vocabulary of emotions and feelings

Set-up

Find a story which is at the correct level for your class. This could be a short text from a news source, a fairytale or a traditional story from a particular culture.

Steps

☐ Tell the learners that you are going to give them a story to read:
- □ You read it aloud and they follow along, reading it.
- □ Alternatively, they read it on their own.

☐ Ask them to note down random feelings or emotions that came up while reading or listening:
- □ They then call out the words they wrote down.
- □ The rest of the class guess which part of the story these words refer to.

☐ Discuss the impact of the story with the learners and compare what the different learners got out of it.

☐ Ask the class if they learned anything new from the story, or if there was anything useful for their own lives in it.

▼

The learners can look for stories to bring to class:
- □ If you have people from different cultures, you can ask them for traditional stories that they could share.
- □ These can be given out as homework, and the learners write sentences about their feelings regarding the stories.

The stories, and what the learners write about them, can then be included in a personal portfolio.

Style spectrum

- Searching for a story is enjoyed by Expert Investigators.
- Finding useful tips or facts in a story is something Power Planners enjoy.
- Calling out their guesses about emotions is something Radical Reformers enjoy.

All about my partner

Strategy
The learners complete sentences based on how they think a partner would answer.

Spotlight on style
Flexible Friend

Spotlight on language
Gerund/infinitive; present simple tense

Set-up

Copy the stem sentences below for the class.

Steps

☐ Put the learners into pairs and give each learner a copy of the stem sentences:
- □ I am good/bad at …
- □ My favourite morning drink is …
- □ I usually like to … at weekends.
- □ I'm afraid of …
- □ I often wear the colour … because …
- □ When I was a child, I wanted to be a/an …
- □ I usually … when I go on holiday.
- □ My friends like to spend time with me because …

☐ The learners fill them out as if they were their partner.

☐ They then exchange papers and discuss which sentences are correct.

☐ Finally, tell them to explain to their partners why they chose what they did.

▼

The learners can write a short story about their partners:
- □ They incorporate the various aspects of the completed stem sentences.
- □ They should elaborate as much as possible.

These can then be read in class or they can be distributed randomly, and the class has to guess who the story is about.

(This activity is based on an idea from Jill Hadfield in *Classroom Dynamics* published by OUP.)

Style spectrum

- Basing a story on facts is something Expert Investigators enjoy.
- Justifying answers is enjoyed by Power Planners.
- Guessing information about someone is something Radical Reformers enjoy

Personal mindmaps

Strategy
The learners work as a group to ask each other about their personal mindmaps, and then introduce each other to the class.

Spotlight on style
Flexible Friend

Spotlight on language
Personal information; dates; hobbies

Steps

☐ Draw *your* personal mindmap on the board. Put your name in the centre circle and draw lines from it.

☐ Write important words, years and names at the end of the lines:
- The learners ask you questions about the mindmap and what the information means.
- You answer the questions.

☐ Put the learners into pairs.

☐ Tell them to each draw their own mindmap. For example:

☐ They then ask each other questions to find out what information is suggested by the mindmap.

☐ When the groups have finished, they take turns introducing each other to the class.

You can tell the learners to take home one of the mindmaps belonging to another person and write a short story about that person's life, using the information. (You can give them a word limit, depending on their level.)
- These can be displayed in the classroom.
- The person whose mindmap was the basis for the story reads it and gives feedback on how accurately it actually portrays them.

Style spectrum

- Being exact is something Expert Investigators enjoy.
- Having clear instructions for the assignment is something Power Planners enjoy.
- Writing a creative story is enjoyed by Radical Reformers.

What we have in common

Strategy
The learners work with a partner to find things they have in common.

Spotlight on style
Flexible Friend

Spotlight on language
Free-time activities; likes and dislikes; goals; gerunds

Set-up

You need to make copies of the stem sentences below.

Steps

☐ Put the learners into pairs and give each one a copy of the stem sentences:
- We both …
- Neither of us has …
- Our families …
- Our plans for the future include …
- We hope to …
- Both of us enjoy …
- Both of us dislike …
- Neither of us likes to …
- If we could, we would …

☐ Ask them to talk to their partners and fill them out.

☐ To find out which pairs had the most in common, they read some of the statements aloud. Do others in the class have the same things in common?

Rather than giving out a prepared set of sentences, the learners can be put into pairs to find five things they have in common.
- Give the pairs five minutes for this activity and tell them that, once they have found five things, they can continue to see how many *other* things they have in common.
- Remind them that they can talk about things in the past, present or future, hobbies, likes, dislikes, free-time activities, etc.

Style spectrum

- Getting details is something Expert Investigators enjoy.
- Organising their time is something Power Planners enjoy.
- Having freedom to find commonalities is something Radical Reformers enjoy.

The perfect page

Strategy
The learners correct common errors.

Spotlight on style
Expert Investigator

Spotlight on language
Common errors: spelling, tenses, prepositions

Set-up

Put together a page of common mistakes that the learners make. These can be taken from written homework or exams. Copy the page for all the learners.

Steps

☐ Give each of the learners the page and ask them to find and correct the mistakes.
  ☐ Go over the answers in open class.
  ☐ Make sure each person writes down the correct answer.

☐ Tell the learners that these are mistakes that they will no longer be making – as they now know the correct forms.

☐ Tell them to use this page when doing homework – to double-check their work.

▼

This can be expanded into ongoing peer correction:
☐ The learners write something in class, as usual.
☐ A partner uses the 'perfect page' to make corrections.

Alternatively, the page is used to look at homework before it is handed in.

The learners can look through corrected homework they get back:
☐ They start their *own* list of corrections which they can add to periodically.
☐ They check with you if they are uncertain about certain corrections.

This can be done after a test by collecting the most common errors the learners made so that they can be worked on.

Style spectrum

- Doing peer correction is enjoyed by Flexible Friends.
- Putting together a list is enjoyed by Power Planners.
- Correcting other people's papers is something enjoyed by Radical Reformers.

Just give me the facts

Strategy
The learners test their knowledge and look up facts after the class.

Spotlight on style
Expert Investigator

Spotlight on language
Comparisons; present and past simple tenses

Set-up

You will need sufficient copies of the 'Facts quiz'.

Steps

☐ Hand out the quiz and ask the learners to work in pairs and guess the correct answers.

☐ Go over the answers in open class.

☐ Encourage the class to check on the facts in the quiz after the class.

☐ While doing so, they should each come up with one or two more questions of their own, which they then ask in a subsequent class.

▼

The class can prepare a facts quiz for another class. This can be themed, depending on the group:
☐ They could look for historical facts, facts about buildings or inventions, or unusual questions about science, etc.
☐ They should bear in mind that they are looking for facts that they think the others probably do not know.

An alternative activity is to ask if statements are *true* or *false*. See the examples for a *true/false* quiz opposite.
☐ Put the learners into pairs and read out your sentences.
☐ The pairs decide, read out their choices and give their reasons for the class to discuss.
For the next lesson, they can research their own statements for the others to guess.

Style spectrum

- Guessing with another person is something enjoyed by Flexible Friends.
- Looking for useful information is something enjoyed by Power Planners.
- Creating a quiz with unusual facts is something enjoyed by Radical Reformers.

Just give me the facts

Facts quiz

1 What is the smallest state and the largest state, in terms of square kilometres, in the USA?

A   Delaware and Texas

B   Rhode Island and Alaska

C   Vermont and California

2 In which European country was the oldest living tree found?

A   Germany

B   Norway

C   Sweden

3 What is the official language of the USA?

A   English

B   None

C   Spanish

4 Which country has the largest number of neighbours?

A   China

B   The Russian Federation

C   Brazil

5 The framework of the Statue of Liberty was designed by the same engineer who designed:

A   The Harbour Bridge in Australia

B   The Guggenheim Museum in New York

C   The Eiffel Tower in Paris

6 The largest empire in the world was:

A   The Roman Empire

B   The Spanish Empire

C   The British Empire

7 The last two times Halley's Comet was seen was in:

A   1910 and 1986

B   1905 and 1981

C   1920 and 2006

8 The largest inland lake in the world is:

A   Lake Victoria

B   Lake Superior

C   The Caspian Sea

Answer key

1   Rhode Island is the smallest (4,002 sq km) and Alaska is the largest (1,717,854 sq km).

2   A Norway spruce discovered in Sweden is said to have started growing at the end of the last Ice Age and has been growing for over 9,550 years.

3   English is the most widely-spread language and is spoken by the government, but the USA has no official language.

4   The country with the largest number of neighbours is China, with 15. The Russian Federation has 14 and Brazil has 10.

5   The Statue of Liberty was constructed in France and given to the USA as a gift. Alexandre Gustave Eiffel designed the steel framework for both the Statue of Liberty and the Eiffel Tower.

6   At one time the British Empire was the largest in the world, covering more than 36 million square kilometres, with a population of between 480 and 570 million people.

7   Halley's Comet was seen in 1910 and 1986. The average period of time of its orbit is 76 years, as predicted in 1705 by Edmond Halley, and it will be seen again at the beginning of 2062.

8   The largest lake is the Caspian Sea (Europe–Asia) which is really a lake as it is surrounded by land, with 386,400 sq km; Lake Superior (North America) is 82,100 sq km and Lake Victoria (Africa) is 69,480 sq km.

True/false quiz

1   *The Pacific is larger than the Atlantic.*

2   *The largest land mammal is the hippopotamus.*

3   *A day has more than 1,500 minutes.*

4   *The first mobile phone call was made in the first half of the twentieth century.*

1   True. The Pacific is larger (155,557,000 sq km) than the Atlantic (76,762,000 sq km).

2   False. The largest land mammal is the African elephant: 4–7 tonnes. The hippopotamus is between 1.4 and 1.5 tonnes.

3   False. A day has 1,440 minutes.

4   True. It was made in 1946.

Nothing but the facts

Strategy
The learners decide on facts related to an article.

Spotlight on style
Expert Investigator

Spotlight on language
Dates: places; mixed tenses

Set-up

Find a current news article (either global or local) in English.

Decide which facts (names, places, dates, etc) to leave out from the article and make cards with this 'missing' information, as well as distractors (cards with *incorrect* information).

Steps

- ☐ Put the learners into small groups and give each group a set of cards.
- ☐ Read your article aloud, leaving blanks where the facts belong.
- ☐ The learners put the cards with the missing words in the correct order.
- ☐ Read the article again, and ask the learners to read the information on their cards.
- ☐ Tell them what the correct answers are.
- ☐ The group with the largest number of correct answers is the winner.

▼

You can encourage the class to look for more information on the topic of the article. They write something up for homework and bring the information to class to discuss in the next lesson.

The learners can write *true/false* statements about the information they have found, and read them aloud for the others to guess.

Style spectrum

- Working in groups with cards is enjoyed by Flexible Friends.
- Deciding on practical information is something enjoyed by Power Planners.
- Writing *true/false* questions for the others is something Radical Reformers enjoy.

Internet investigation

Strategy
The learners gather information from internet sites to talk about in class.

Spotlight on style
Expert Investigator

Spotlight on language
Dates and figures; timelines

Steps

- ☐ Brainstorm on the board areas of interest for the class. These could include, for example:

  sports and sports clubs   *companies*
  holiday destinations   *countries*
  various forms of media   *products*
  music and music groups   *new technology*

- ☐ Find out who is particularly interested in each of the topics and assign one topic to each learner. If you have a large class, more than one person can cover a topic.
- ☐ Brainstorm ideas regarding information the learners would find interesting to know about and write up some of the questions.
- ☐ Tell the learners that their job is to find five facts about their topic:
  - ☐ If possible, they answer the questions they were asked.
  - ☐ Alternatively, they search for information they think no one else will know and bring it to class to present it.

▼

The learners can give a mini-presentation for the class with the information they have discovered.
- ☐ If more than one learner researched the same topic, you can give them some time in class to pool the information before presenting.
- ☐ If presentation software is available in the classroom, the learners can create presentation slides or show the information they have found.

Each topic can be followed by a class discussion, which may lead to further research possibilities.

Style spectrum

- Collaborating with another person is something enjoyed by Flexible Friends.
- Structuring a presentation is enjoyed by Power Planners.
- Discovering interesting facts is something enjoyed by Radical Reformers.

Researching an excursion

Strategy
The learners do internet research to find the best flights, hotel and activities for a class trip.

Spotlight on style
Expert Investigator

Spotlight on language
Travel arrangements: accommodation, sites; mixed tenses

Steps

☐ Give the learners the following information:
  ☐ The class are planning a trip to a large city for a long weekend. (Let them choose the city and the dates.)
  ☐ They would like to see the major sights.
  ☐ They would also like to have an evening out. (Let them choose several activities as options.)

☐ Tell the class that they need to find:
  ☐ the least expensive and most convenient flights
  ☐ the hotel which offers the best value for money
  ☐ the most interesting sights
  ☐ unusual or fun activities to do in the evening

☐ The learners can either use computers or smartphones in class to do the research, or they can do it at home and bring it to class.

☐ They present the information they found, and the class then votes on which of the ideas would suit them all best.

The learners can write a formal proposal for the class excursion. They should use a format which includes:
☐ an introduction
☐ findings
☐ recommendations
☐ a conclusion
These can then be corrected in class.

Style spectrum

- Finding activities to do together is something enjoyed by Flexible Friends.
- Planning the details of a trip is something enjoyed by Power Planners.
- Looking for interesting activities is something enjoyed by Radical Reformers.

How does it work?

Strategy
The learners explain a simple machine or process.

Spotlight on style
Power Planner

Spotlight on language
Sequencing words; passive voice

Set-up

Bring to class a simple mechanical 'machine' (eg a stapler or pencil sharpener).

Steps

☐ Pre-teach any necessary vocabulary, then ask the learners to work in small groups and write out the steps in the passive voice explaining how the machine works.

☐ One of the groups reads their explanation aloud and the others compare it with their own. Correct any mistakes.

☐ Ask the groups to think of a simple machine or process they are familiar with:
  ☐ They write out the steps without mentioning the actual machine or process.
  ☐ The others guess what they have described.

☐ Alternatively, each learner chooses a device to explain to a partner but without saying what it is:
  ☐ The partner writes down each of the steps described to them and asks questions when it is unclear.
  ☐ The partner guesses what the device is.
  ☐ Both partners write out instructions for both devices.

The learners can be assigned specific devices in class or at home – computer programs, mobile phone apps, etc. The others ask for advice, and they teach each other.

Learners who need this type of language for their job can prepare descriptions of more complicated machines or processes. Once their work has been corrected, they give a mini-presentation.

Style spectrum

- Working together is something Flexible Friends enjoy.
- Looking for specific information is something enjoyed by Expert Investigators.
- Writing sentences for a guessing game is enjoyed by Radical Reformers.

Is everything in order?

Strategy
The learners put a process in the correct order.

Spotlight on style
Power Planner

Spotlight on language
Passive voice

Set-up

Find a process which consists of at least eight to ten steps using the passive voice (booking a flight online, setting up features on a mobile phone, a process the learners use at work, etc). Write the steps out and cut them up into cards.

Steps

☐ Put the learners into groups and give each group a set of cards.

☐ Ask them to put the process in order.

☐ When they have finished, ask each of the groups to first make notes on why they chose the order they did.

☐ One of the groups then reads their process aloud and they correct the order in open class.

☐ Open up a discussion about the logic of the correct order, and ask if those with a different order can justify their decisions.

▼

The learners can think of a process *they* know and create a similar activity for another learner:
▫ They write out the process on a piece of paper and exchange it with their partner, who tries to put it into the correct order.
▫ The pairs then discuss the correct order and the justification for it.

They can then add the sequencing words to the process.

Style spectrum

- Working with a partner to complete a task is something Flexible Friends enjoy.
- Ordering processes is enjoyed by Expert Investigators.
- Justifying decisions is enjoyed by Radical Reformers.

Group grammar

Strategy
The learners become aware of how grammar plays a functional role in communication.

Spotlight on style
Power Planner

Spotlight on language
Difficult grammar points

Set-up

Collect common grammar mistakes using tenses which lead to misunderstandings. Find pictures or photographs which help to illustrate these tenses: they can show someone doing something or getting ready to do something, or something has been done or hasn't yet been done.

Steps

☐ Put the learners into small groups and give each group a set of pictures or photographs.

☐ Write up on the board the tenses you want to practise.

☐ The learners use the different tenses to describe the photos and write each of them on a separate piece of paper:
▫ They leave the photographs and the pieces of paper with the tenses on their desks.
▫ They then move to the right, to the next group, and match the statements to the pictures.

☐ Tell them to go back to their original places and check what the others have done.

☐ Check the results in open class and discuss any problems.

☐ Go over the grammar rules so that everyone understands why the tenses they used were the correct ones, or not.

▼

The learners can look for a photograph they like in a magazine or on the internet and write sentences about it:
▫ You give them the tenses you would like them to practise.
▫ They then bring their photos to class and show the others while reading the sentences, before discussing the tenses.

Style spectrum

- Finding photographs they like is something enjoyed by Flexible Friends.
- Looking for rules is something Expert Investigators enjoy.
- Moving about the class is enjoyed by Radical Reformers.

Confirming information

Strategy
The learners brainstorm information they think will be in a text and then read the text to confirm it.

Spotlight on style
Power Planner

Spotlight on language
Vocabulary; mixed tenses

Set-up

You need to make copies of the text you are going to use.

Steps

☐ Choose a text which will be of interest to your learners – about a famous person, a city, a building, a film, etc.

☐ Tell the learners the topic of the text.

☐ Put them into pairs or groups and ask them to come up with as many words or as much information as possible that they think will be in the text.

☐ Collect the ideas on the board.

☐ Hand out the text and ask the learners to take turns reading it aloud.

☐ When they come across vocabulary or ideas they had predicted, they underline it in the text.

☐ The pair or group with the most vocabulary or ideas wins.

Using the text as a basis, you can put the learners into three groups, each with a different task. If the class is too large for three groups to work comfortably, each of these groups can be divided into smaller groups to work on the text.
◻ Group 1 writes five comprehension questions about it.
◻ Group 2 writes five definitions of vocabulary found in it.
◻ Group 3 writes five discussion questions about it.
The groups then pass their questions or definitions to the next group who answers them.
Finish up with a general discussion of the text.

Style spectrum

- Collaborating is something Flexible Friends enjoy.
- Looking for details and writing questions is something Expert Investigators enjoy.
- Creating questions for others is something enjoyed by Radical Reformers.

Setting priorities

Strategy
The learners work on their own to set priorities in organising a class celebration.

Spotlight on style
Power Planner

Spotlight on language
Future tenses

Steps

☐ Choose a future event which the class is interested in. This can include: a year-end activity, an evening out at the end of the course, an excursion, preparing for a final exam, etc.

☐ Brainstorm different aspects of the organisation of the event or activity with the learners:
   ◻ They work on their own to decide on the order of the steps to be followed.
   ◻ They set their own priorities.

☐ Compare the order in open class.

☐ Ask the learners to explain how they decided which steps were *most* or *least* important.

The learners can each choose a general topic in the news and set out priorities for working on it.
◻ They bring their ideas to class and present them to the others.
◻ Run a general class discussion on the ideas of the different learners and compare their lists.
◻ Discuss the reasons for the priorities they set – they need to find arguments for their decisions.
◻ This could be expanded into a debate in which the learners are encouraged to offer unique solutions or options.
This could also be done with one particular news topic, or by assigning the same news topic to several learners rather than letting them choose different ones – in order to make more exact comparisons.

Style spectrum

- Planning a group activity is enjoyed by Flexible Friends.
- Determining the importance of steps is enjoyed by Expert Investigators.
- Finding unique solutions or options is something enjoyed by Radical Reformers.

Linking ideas

Strategy
The learners use linking phrases
to structure spoken discourse.

Spotlight on style
Power Planner

Spotlight on language
Linking words and phrases

Set-up

Copy and cut up the 'linking words' cards opposite.

Steps

☐ Put the learners into groups, give each group a set of
cards and ask them to turn them face down.

☐ Brainstorm some topics of interest with the class and
write them on the board:
  ▫ The learners choose a topic.
  ▫ They say one or two sentences.
  ▫ They then pick up a linking word card and continue –
    using the word they have chosen.

☐ Another person in the group then continues with the
topic, taking a linking word after one or two sentences.

☐ This continues until the linking words have all been used.

The learners can use the linking words to write an article
or story on the topic – this can be done as homework or as
groupwork in class. They can then carry out peer correction,
giving each other reasons for their comments.

(I learned this activity from Tina Črepnik-Schmidt.)

before	during	because
although	but	and
when	however	even though
since	in addition	while
so	or	after
whether or not	nevertheless	in spite of
as well	furthermore	in the meantime
so that	in order to	therefore
as a result	consequently	resulting in
in order not to	in contrast to	having said that
for example	for instance	despite
as soon as	subsequently	in other words

Style spectrum

- Taking part in a group discussion is something enjoyed
  by Flexible Friends.
- Deciding how to continue a sentence logically is enjoyed
  by Expert Investigators.
- Coming up with interesting ideas is something enjoyed
  by Radical Reformers.

Radical roleplay

Strategy
The learners speak freely in a roleplay.

Spotlight on style
Radical Reformer

Spotlight on language
Giving directions; recommending something; asking for help

Set-up

Copy and cut up the role cards opposite for each group of six learners.

Steps

- [ ] Put learners into groups of six.
- [ ] Tell them to decide which city they are in – the group has to agree on one.
- [ ] Give each of the learners a role card and ask them to remember what is on it.
- [ ] Explain that the person they ask might not have the information they need and they will have to ask another person.
- [ ] The learners do their roleplay in their groups.
- [ ] After they have finished, one group can enact theirs again for the class.
- [ ] Find out what language the learners needed, and brainstorm phrases together.
- [ ] They can then repeat the roleplay, taking on new roles and using the new phrases.

▼

You can ask the learners if they have ever been in the situation described opposite:

- Discuss the experiences they have had.
- Ask them to write out dialogues for homework.
- Correct them in the next lesson.

> You are a tourist in town. You don't have a guidebook with you so you ask people on the street if they can recommend interesting sights.

> You are very proud of several of the sights in town. You can explain these in detail if someone asks you about them, and tell them exactly how to get there.

> You are a tourist in town and are looking for a good restaurant with traditional food. Ask people if they can recommend one.

> Your favourite restaurant is closed but there is another place you have been meaning to try. It is a bit complicated to find, however.

> You are lost and trying to find a particular building. You are late for an appointment there. Ask the people you see where it is.

> You are not from here and don't really know where things are. But the tourist office is nearby and they have always been very helpful.

Style spectrum

- Giving exact information is something enjoyed by Expert Investigators.
- Helping someone is something Flexible Friends enjoy.
- Recommending is enjoyed by Power Planners.

Act out the characters

Strategy
The learners speak freely and act out characters
from a story.

Spotlight on style
Radical Reformer

Spotlight on language
Mixed vocabulary; mixed tenses

Set-up

Copy the story opposite for the class. This story is based on one that appeared in *The New York Times* some 25 years ago.

Steps

☐ Hand out the story and ask the learners to read it.

☐ Tell them that they are going to act out four different scenarios:
  ▫ Officer Carrol being interviewed by a reporter.
  ▫ Officer Carrol paying a call on Johnny's parents.
  ▫ Johnny's parents talking to Johnny about his adventure.
  ▫ Johnny bragging about his adventure to his friends the next day.

☐ The learners decide if they would like to play a role and which scene they would like to act out.

☐ They should think about the details of the story, and how they can incorporate them into the roleplay and elaborate on them. If details are missing, they should come up with ones which make sense to them.

☐ Give them some time to work on their roleplays, and then ask them to perform in front of the class.

▼

The learners can look for an interesting short story in the news.
  ▫ They choose some of the people in the story to write dialogues about.
  ▫ They then bring the dialogues to class and act out the characters, as above.

Style spectrum

- Deciphering the details of a story is something enjoyed by Expert Investigators.
- Roleplaying in a group is enjoyed by Flexible Friends.
- Organising a roleplay is something Power Planners enjoy.

The lure of the road

One day, a young man decided to take a drive with his sister. There were two problems with this idea, however. First of all, he didn't have a driver's license and, secondly, he couldn't see over the steering wheel. Johnny, five years old, took the keys from his mother's handbag and invited his little sister, Sabrina, for a ride. He carefully backed the car out of the driveway and headed towards town. Greg Carrol, a local policeman, saw the car and thought that an invisible person must be driving it.

So Officer Carrol turned on his siren and the car pulled over to the curb and stopped. To Officer Carrol's surprise, he saw a young boy in pajamas and a little girl in just a pajama top in the back seat. He told Johnny that he would have to call his mother to pick them up but Johnny told him that she was ill and his dad was at work. He added that they only had one car and he could drive home and then bring his mother to the station, as he was already an experienced driver.

Can you sell it?

Strategy
The learners choose an everyday item
and try to sell it to the other learners.

Spotlight on style
Radical Reformer

Spotlight on language
Language of recommendations and persuasion

Steps

☐ Tell the learners that they are going to sell something in the room (paper clip, pen, pencil case, remote control, etc).

☐ Divide the class into *buyers* and *sellers*.

☐ Tell the sellers to choose one item and decide how much it costs (set a limit on the price for everyone – eg up to 50 Euros) and what is special about the item, being as specific as possible.
  - ☐ Tell the buyers they each have 50 Euros to spend.
  - ☐ Tell the sellers to sell as many of their item as they can.
  - ☐ Tell the class that it is possible to negotiate discounts but the buyers can only spend the allotted amount.

☐ Set a time limit, then stop the class and find out who bought what.

☐ Hold a 'debriefing' session, asking why the buyers bought the items they bought, thinking about the following questions if they bought an item:
  - ☐ Was it because the relationship with the seller was important?
  - ☐ Was it because they needed the item itself?

The learners can think about the conversations they had as buyer or seller:
- ☐ They write out a dialogue at home and look up any vocabulary they think is necessary.
- ☐ You then correct the dialogues in class.

Repeat the activity, switching roles: the buyers are now the sellers, and vice-versa. Did the learners find any difference in the conversations – after working on the dialogues individually?

Style spectrum

- Looking for details is enjoyed by Expert Investigators.
- Creating relationships is enjoyed by Flexible Friends.
- Negotiating is something Power Planners enjoy.

The restaurant game

Strategy
The learners act out roles of people in a restaurant.

Spotlight on style
Radical Reformer

Spotlight on language
Foods and how foods are prepared; words for service

Set-up

Find pictures of food and put them on cards. Also find a typical menu that contains some examples of the pictures, and make enough copies for the 'customers'.

Steps

☐ Divide the class into *cooks*, *servers* and *customers*. The cooks need an area to work in – the kitchen; the customers need to sit at tables – the restaurant.
  - ☐ The cooks are given food pictures which they organise into categories found on menus (starters, main courses, beverages, etc).
  - ☐ Meanwhile, the servers bring menus to the customers, answer questions about the food and take the orders.

☐ The servers go to the kitchen and tell the cooks the orders:
  - ☐ The cooks give them the appropriate pictures.
  - ☐ If something was ordered that they don't have, they give the servers something else.

☐ The servers go back to the customers and 'serve' the meal, by laying the pictures in front of them:
  - ☐ If the server had to bring something the customer did not order, they try and convince them to accept the substitution, or they offer something else that the kitchen does have.
  - ☐ If the customer is not satisfied, the server may have to offer a free beverage or dessert.

☐ At the end of the game, the customers ask for the bill – which the server then brings.

The learners can write their own menus, to be used instead.

Style spectrum

- Explaining exactly how something was prepared is something Expert Investigators enjoy.
- Roleplaying in a restaurant is enjoyed by Flexible Friends.
- Telling someone to take what they haven't ordered is something enjoyed by Power Planners.

When I was a child ...

Strategy
The learners write sentences about their past beliefs.

Spotlight on style
Radical Reformer

Spotlight on language
Used to; past tense

Steps

☐ Write three sentences up on the board, using the stem:
When I was a child … .
Two of the sentences should be true and one should be false. For example:
When I was a child, I used to believe that brown cows produced chocolate milk.
When I was a child, I used to believe that my teachers slept at school.
When I was a child, I used to believe in the tooth fairy.

☐ Ask the learners which one they think is false.

☐ Tell the learners which of your sentences *was* false.

☐ Put the learners into groups of four or five and tell them to each write three sentences, one of which is false:
  ▫ They read their sentences to each other and ask the others which one they think is false.
  ▫ For each correct guess, the learners get one point.
  ▫ If no one guesses the false sentence, the person who wrote it gets two points.

☐ Add up the points at the end of the game.

▼

The learners can look for interesting ideas on the internet about what people used to believe. They can be given a specific period in history or famous people to research.
▫ They bring their findings to class and share the information.
▫ This can be developed into a further discussion of superstitions and what different cultures believe is true.
They could also find facts to bring to class for the others to guess when these particular facts were believed to be true.
For example: *People used to believe the world was flat.*

Style spectrum

- Looking for historical facts is something enjoyed by Expert Investigators.
- Finding out what others believed as children is something Flexible Friends enjoy.
- Organising a discussion is enjoyed by Power Planners.

Our ideal home

Strategy
The learners work in groups to design a home for all of them to live in.

Spotlight on style
Radical Reformer

Spotlight on language
Vocabulary about homes

Set-up

You will need paper and pens for the learners to design their homes.

Steps

☐ Brainstorm different rooms in a house and areas (city, country, seaside, mountains) in which homes are located.

☐ Ask the learners to talk about the places they live and what they like about them.

☐ Put the learners into groups and tell them they are going to design a home where they will live together.

☐ Tell them that money is no object but they must design a place where each of them will be comfortable.
  ▫ Give them time to plan and discuss it together.
  ▫ Give out paper, pens and flipchart paper, and ask the learners to make a poster by drawing their ideal homes.

☐ When they have finished, they present their designs to the others and answer any questions.

☐ The group can then decide which of the homes was the most interesting, comfortable, best place to visit, etc.

▼

This can be prepared at home by asking the learners to find photos or pictures to bring to class or do research on different building styles, energy-saving homes, etc. Then they can prepare their posters using the photos.

As a final assignment, they can write an essay on their ideal home, and what they especially like about it.

Style spectrum

- Doing research on the internet for information is something enjoyed by Expert Investigators.
- Creating a space to live with others is something enjoyed by Flexible Friends.
- Planning a practical home is enjoyed by Power Planners.

The department store

Strategy
The learners roleplay shopping in a large store.

Spotlight on style
Mixed

Spotlight on language
Everyday items; departments in a big store

Set-up

You need blank cards on which you write several shopping situations (you need a birthday present, clothes for a job interview, things to take on a two-week cruise to Asia, for a surprise party for someone in your office, etc). Find photos of various items found in department stores (in adverts or catalogues, etc). You also need additional blank cards.

Steps

☐ Ask the learners to name departments in large stores.

☐ The departments that will be used in the game are then written on cards and placed around the classroom.

☐ Sort the items into the correct department. If there are no prices on the photos, the learners have to price them.

☐ Several learners will be *salespeople*, the others *shoppers*.
  ☐ The shoppers are given a limit of money and a situation card, and told to make a list and buy what they think will be most appropriate, unusual or fun.
  ☐ The salespeople try to sell as much as they can and keep track of their sales, while the shoppers try to keep within their limit – but buy everything they need.

☐ A final debriefing includes the items that were bought – and why they were bought.

The salespeople can elaborate on what they could have sold but didn't have in stock. The buyers can explain why they bought one item but not another. This can be done orally or in writing.

Style spectrum

- Talking to others is something Flexible Friends enjoy.
- Deciding what an item costs is something Expert Investigators enjoy.
- Making a list is something Power Planners enjoy.
- Looking for unusual or fun items to buy is something Radical Reformers enjoy.

Our type of trip

Strategy
The learners work in their style groups and plan an activity.

Spotlight on style
Mixed

Spotlight on language
Travel words; tourist sights

Set-up

You need to know the preferred Mind Organisation styles of your learners. You will also need a flipchart, paper and pens.

Steps

☐ Put the learners into groups according to their preferred Mind Organisation style.

☐ Tell them that they have to plan an overnight trip to some place that is interesting for the class.
  ☐ Give them a budget, and explain that they need to stay within it. They may need to do some research for this.
  ☐ Give each of the groups a piece of flipchart paper, pens and a time limit of 15–20 minutes to plan.

☐ Ask each group to present their ideas to the class.

☐ The class choose one of the destinations and give their reasons for their choice.

You can 'debrief' after this activity – to find out how the groups went about their planning. For example:
  ☐ How did the group decide where to go?
  ☐ How did they organise the trip?
Comparing the different styles of organisation:
  ☐ Did the different groups work in different ways?
  ☐ Did they go about the task in a similar way?
Working together:
  ☐ How could the ideas be combined into one plan?
  ☐ Which compromises would they need to make?

Style spectrum

- Collaborating is something Flexible Friends enjoy.
- Determining details about finances is something Expert Investigators enjoy.
- Organising an activity is something Power Planners enjoy.
- Thinking up something interesting to do is something Radical Reformers enjoy.

Don't say the word!

Strategy
The learners create their own 'taboo' cards
and play a game.

Spotlight on style
Mixed

Spotlight on language
Vocabulary which has been covered in class

Set-up

You will need blank cards for each group of learners.

Steps

☐ Divide the class into four groups and hand out some blank cards.

☐ Assign each group a topic or word which has been covered in class. For example:
  □ hobbies
  □ food
  □ holidays
  Alternatively, you can ask the learners to choose the topic or word themselves.

☐ Get each group to write down the topic/word on a card and to write underneath five words or short phrases which *must not* be used in talking about the topic/word on the card:

  These are 'taboo'. See the examples opposite.

☐ When the group has created their card, this is given to another group.

☐ This group has two minutes to explain their topic/word to the other groups *without using* the taboo words or phrases.

☐ The group that chose the taboo words have to listen carefully, to make sure that none of them are used:
  □ If any *are* used, the group explaining gets no points.
  □ If one of the other groups guesses the topic/word, both they *and* the group describing it get one point.

☐ Add up the points at the end.

Style spectrum

- Playing a game together is enjoyed by Flexible Friends.
- Coming up with details is enjoyed by Expert Investigators.
- Choosing 'taboo' words is enjoyed by Power Planners.
- Looking for unusual information is something enjoyed by Radical Reformers.

Topic: *New York City*	Topic: *Free-time activities*
Taboo:	**Taboo:**
■ *Empire State Building*	■ *Leisure*
■ *Broadway*	■ *Sports*
■ *Hudson River*	■ *Weekend*
■ *Rockefeller Center*	■ *Holidays*
■ *East Coast*	■ *Fun*

The topics can then be used for short articles for a class magazine. These can be written in class or at home.

The learners can find appropriate photos, pictures or drawings to make the articles look like they belong in a magazine, as well as facts and unusual information which have not been covered in class.

□ These can be used for a class portfolio or displayed in the classroom.
□ The unusual information or additional facts could be used for a further guessing game as well. ·

My first time ...

Strategy
The learners write a story about a 'first time' event in their lives which was important to them.

Spotlight on style
Mixed

Spotlight on language
Past tenses

Steps

☐ Give the learners a questionnaire with questions about 'firsts'. See the examples opposite.

☐ Ask them to interview each other in pairs:
   - ☐ If their partner gives them an answer to the question, they should ask for more details – using the other question words and creating appropriate questions.
   - ☐ If their partner says they don't remember, they move on to another event.

☐ Follow up this questionnaire by asking the learners to write a short story about an important first in their lives.

☐ If possible, they should look for a photo of themselves from that time.

☐ They bring in the story and their photo and share the story with the others in the class.

▼

A variation is for each learner to write a childhood story:
- ☐ The learners then print out their stories and attach their childhood photos to them.
- ☐ They hang them up around the classroom and the others walk around the room reading the stories and guessing who they belong to.
- ☐ The stories can be numbered, allowing each learner to write a list of names.
- ☐ They say whose story they think each one belongs to.
- ☐ The writers then reveal their identities.

When was the first time ...
- you went to school by yourself?
- you rode a bicycle?
- you played a sport in a team?
- you swam in the sea?
- you travelled to another country?
- you travelled by plane?
- you fell in love?
- you lost something important?
- you stayed up all night?
- you went to a party?
- you baked a cake?
- you went on holiday with friends?
- you went to a circus, theatre performance or concert?
- you learned a foreign language?

If your partner can remember an event, ask more questions using these words and making notes:

What ... ?

Why ...?

How ...?

Who ...?

Where ...?

(The activity is based on one I learned from Kurt Scheibner in *Ready-made English 1*, published by Heinemann. I got the idea for the activity variation from a talk given by Leni Dam at an IATEFL LASIG conference.)

Style spectrum

- Discovering things about others is something enjoyed by Flexible Friends.
- Asking for details is enjoyed by Expert Investigators.
- Deciding is something Power Planners enjoy.
- Writing a unique story is enjoyed by Radical Reformers.

Your last chance

Strategy
The learners work in groups to save the human race.

Spotlight on style
Mixed

Spotlight on language
Language of persuasion and justification

Set-up

You need to know the preferred Mind Organisation styles of your learners. Copy the instructions opposite.

Steps

☐ Put the class into groups of six to 10 learners, consisting of people with different Mind Organisation profiles.

☐ Give them the instructions and say they have 45 minutes to come to an agreement.

☐ When they have finished, give the groups these questions:
  ☐ Which arguments were logical? Emotional? Unusual?
  ☐ How did they decide within the group?
  ☐ Were there group leaders, or did they take part equally?

☐ Each of the groups present their findings to the class and talk about the questions.

☐ Lead a general class discussion on the findings – on the way *different* learner types work together.

▼

This activity can also be carried out by forming groups of the *same* Mind Organisation profile.
The questions above can be extended:
☐ Was it comfortable working with those of the same profile? Why? Why not?
☐ How did they organise the activity?
Lead a discussion on the way *similar* types work together.

(I learned this activity from Brigitte Jug.)

> **The earth is about to be destroyed, and six people will be chosen to go to another planet to continue the human race.**
>
> Choose from the following:
> - a 35-year-old man: a well-respected religious leader
> - a 65-year-old female doctor
> - a forty-year-old male painter and a 25-year-old female writer in a wheelchair who will only travel together
> - a 20-year-old female student who does not like authority
> - a 55-year-old male carpenter
> - a 30-year-old male who has never had a job
> - a 45-year-old female diplomat

Style spectrum

- Deciding on a final result together is something enjoyed by Flexible Friends.
- Being logical is something Expert Investigators enjoy.
- Organising how an activity should be done is enjoyed by Power Planners.
- Coming up with ideas or suggestions is something Radical Reformers enjoy.

Spotlight on Learning Styles has so far presented and explained three learning style models, provided checklists for you and your students to discover which type of learners you are, and offered a range of activities which can be adapted to a number of teaching situations and classes.

- **Part A** looked at styles from the point of view of both the learner and the teacher in order to clarify not only how our learners learn but how we ourselves teach, finishing off with a discussion of what styles are and what they are *not* – and the implications of learning styles in our teaching.

  Spotlight on styles gave details of these three different models and pointed out the characteristics of learners and teachers and their style preferences.

- **Part B** suggested a wealth of activities which spotlighted each of the models, while the 'Style spectrum' showed how *all* learners and *all* preferences are still being catered for.

  Spotlight on strategies, the first chapter, included checklists for both learners and teachers – as well as practical suggestions for the different learner and teacher styles.

So a question remains: *Where can you go from here?*

The hope is that, by finding out about your style and those of your learners, *you* have discovered how to make the activities work effectively – while observing how the *learners* approached them and carried them out.

Also, the concept of stretching into other styles may be the missing piece of the puzzle that learners have been seeking. Helping them to understand themselves, and how they are most comfortable perceiving and organising information, can help broaden their horizons and give them the motivation to go on exploring for themselves.

Although there are a multitude of different learning style models, it was necessary to make a choice of what to present – three models were ultimately chosen for this book. However, it is important to demonstrate that there are *other* approaches to learning styles which can help us to discover how learners learn best.

Delving into the concept of learning styles and looking at classroom work from that point of view should offer a starting point for *further* observation and investigation.

| Further approaches | Further activities | Further reading |

This, then, is the direction in which we shall be going in Part C.

Learning and teaching

As mentioned in Part A, we have the opportunity to either *harmonise* with our learners or to *challenge* them. Both of these approaches have value and can be used to reach different goals:

- When we look for activities which appeal to the predominant learning styles of our learners, we create an atmosphere which will make them feel comfortable and help them succeed as learners. However, there is no guarantee that everything they need to learn will be presented in the way in which they feel happiest learning.
- When we add the element of challenge, therefore, we assist our learners to stretch out of their comfort zones and we encourage them to discover new techniques and develop their own learning strategies.

In other words, when we *first* harmonise with them to establish a basis for learning and *then* challenge them to learn in new ways, we have the opportunity to provide them with skills for life-long learning.

This philosophy applies to teachers as well. Most of us are comfortable *teaching* in the way in which we enjoy *learning*. However, we may be mismatching a group of learners in our classrooms and not fulfilling everyone's needs. By trying out activities which appeal to different styles:

- We begin to see not only *how* something can be done, taught or practised.
- We also begin to see *how else* something can be done, taught or practised.

We are thereby offered the chance for professional development on a level which we may not have considered earlier.

Looking back

If you have done some of the activities in Part B by now, or when you do, take some time to think back over them and your reactions to them:

What are *your* conclusions?
- What went right? Why did it work?
- What went wrong? Why didn't it work?
- What can you improve or change?
- Did you find the activities changed your outlook in any way?
- Were many of them familiar, or were they different to your usual style?
- How easy or difficult was it to incorporate these ideas into your teaching?
- Do you think you are more tolerant of learners with styles different to your own?

What are your *learners'* conclusions?
- Did they discover new aspects of their learning habits?
- Did they begin to understand their individual needs and strengths better?
- Did they feel the information helped them become more autonomous and/or motivated?

So the question appears again: *Where can you go from here?*

Looking forward

These reflections are meant as food for thought in your own future personal development as a teacher, trainer, counsellor, etc. The aim here is to encourage you to go back and think about the ideas that were presented and individualise them, as everyone approaches these types of questions differently. Perhaps you will gain a different insight from a colleague, or you may find that you agree with some aspects and not with others. And therein lies the beauty of differentiated learning and teaching.

Our brains continue to learn and change – as long as we provide the stimulus for this growth. Therefore, implementing ideas which may seem foreign at first can become the most stimulating part of our teaching. Much of what we do is routine, but trying out something new – even if it feels strange or uncomfortable at first – can be the way to expand our skills and talents and reawaken our huge potential for creativity:

From spotlight to springboard

Further approaches

Although there are a multitude of different learning style models, it was necessary to make a choice of what to present – three models were chosen for this book. According to Andrew D. Cohen in 'Focus on the Language Learner: Styles, Strategies and Motivation' – his contribution to *An Introduction to Applied Linguistics*, edited by Norbert Schmitt:

'Researchers both in educational psychology and the L2 field have observed that various learners approach learning in a significantly different manner, and the concept of 'learning styles' has been used to refer to these differences. ... Although numerous distinctions are emerging from the literature, three categories of style preferences are considered particularly relevant and useful to understanding the process of language learning: sensory/perceptual, cognitive and personality-related preferences.'

For the reason Cohen mentions above, our three models were chosen as follows:
- Sensory perception – explored in the modality research carried out by Drs Swassing and Barbe – was the logical start.
- The second model mentioned by Cohen – the cognitive processing studies by Witkin – presented itself as the best follow-up.
- The behavioural studies by Bowie were chosen to round off the models as helpful aids for language learners and teachers.

However, as we have said, there are other approaches to learning styles which can also provide us with further valuable information and possibilities in our attempts to discover how to help our learners learn to the best of their abilities.

The quotes below correspond to expert researchers, a selection of whose works are to be found in 'Further reading' on page 114.

Experiential Learning

Businesspeople, people in adult education and some language teachers may be familiar with David Kolb's experiential model of learning. I myself was introduced to this model in a teacher training seminar by Jim Wingate, and I used it for many years in ELT courses for adult learners.

In the early 1970s, Kolb – an expert in the field of management – developed a model based on empirical evidence, and in 1971 created a 'learning styles inventory' (known as the Kolb LSI) to enable people to determine their learning preferences. Kolb felt that there were two major dimensions in learning: namely, how people perceive and how they process information.

Like Gregorc's and Bowie's models, Kolb determined that perception first takes place either concretely or abstractly. However, in Kolb's model, emotions and feelings fall under the umbrella of 'concrete perception', rather than 'abstract' as in Gregorc and Bowie.

The second part of his model dealt with the processing of information and, here, Kolb divided this into those who use *observation* and those who actively *experiment* with new things they learn. This also created four distinct learning styles – four quadrants:
- Type One learners – who perceive concretely and process reflectively. These learners need to be personally involved and look at complicated concepts from different perspectives.
- Type Two learners – who perceive abstractly and process reflectively. These learners depend on theories and tend to test any theories they find for illogicality.
- Type Three learners – who perceive abstractly and process through active experimentation. These learners focus on solving specific problems by using hypothetical and deductive reasoning in order to find a way to implement practical ideas.
- Type Four learners – who perceive concretely and process through active experimentation. These learners look for new experiences and tend to learn by trial and error.

Kolb's theory was that each of these four learner types developed their own patterns and

'When it is used in the simple, straightforward and open way intended, the LSI usually provides an interesting self-examination and discussion that recognizes the uniqueness, complexity and variability in individual approaches to learning.'
David Kolb

strategies for learning. He also felt that the experiential learning cycle comprised of the four types is an ongoing process in which learners test and retest ideas to make them fit their experience. By combining abstract theories, such as grammar rules, and concrete situations, such as roleplays, with reflection and active experimentation, individuals have the opportunity to think about what they have learned and then to actively try it out.

In addition, Kolb felt that learning was dependent on the goals and aims of the individual, and that what people learned needed to be relevant to them. As goals and aims differ from person to person, this has an effect on the way people learn and how they approach tasks, adding another individual touch to learner strategies and actions.

The 4MAT® System

In 1979, Bernice McCarthy, a teacher educator, developed a system using Kolb's learning styles to demonstrate how teachers could best create lessons by building in elements from the quadrants.
- She began with the Type One quadrant, feeling that information needed to be presented in a way in which learners could find a personal connection to it and understand the reason for learning.
- She then moved on to the Type Two quadrant, feeling that this was the best place to provide learners with the rules and background.
- The Type Three quadrant was then the best area to begin guided practice.
- In the Type Four quadrant, learners would be ready to experiment on their own.

'The 4MAT® system is a model for teaching. It seems to work at all ages and with all subject matter. It is based on my belief that everyone can learn.'
Bernice McCarthy

McCarthy called this the '4MAT® System' and offered a number of examples for different school subjects to be taught in this way. She also stressed that the final quadrant of actively experimenting with learned material was the place to find out if learners needed more work on one of the other areas of presentation; and that parts of the cycle could be repeated.

Although this system is not limited to teaching languages, then, it can be used effectively in the language classroom, as demonstrated in the following example:

An aspect of English teaching which can be difficult to get across is the concept and use of the present perfect tense, as it may not exist in the learners' first language.
- Therefore, making it personal can be achieved by having a student come to the front of the room and instructing them to ask the question: *'How long are you here?'* The teacher then answers with a number of different responses, including: *'I am staying for two more weeks'* and *'I will be here altogether for three weeks'*. The learners then begin to understand that there is a reason for learning this tense – as *native* speakers simply do not know how to answer the question posed to them.
- In the second quadrant, the teacher explains what the present perfect is and when it is used. This can vary according to the level of the class, and include simple rules and signal words or be explained in more detail.

'To learn successfully, a student also needs expertise in other learning styles; together these styles form a natural cycle of learning.'
Bernice McCarthy

- The third quadrant lends itself to drills and practice. This can be done by setting up gap texts or a 'Find someone who has …' activity which is then checked by the teacher.
- The last quadrant is then used to practise more freely. Here, the learners can be given a roleplay using the present perfect, or be asked to write their own questions to ask the others. In this quadrant, the role of the teacher involves monitoring the language and, if necessary, going back to one of the earlier quadrants to explain the rules again or explicitly drill the structure of the tense.

In this cycle, all the styles are included so that everyone has a chance to 'harmonise' and 'be challenged'. Learners who are stronger in one aspect than another can help fellow students in a peer-to-peer fashion if necessary.

Further approaches

Multiple Intelligences

'All children are gifted. Every child is a unique human being – a very special person.'
Thomas Armstrong

Multiple Intelligences, which were first identified in the early 1980s by Howard Gardner, are sometimes referred to as 'styles' although, in my experience working with them, they seem to fall more into the category of *talents*. They are also generally set at an early age, although they may change to some degree and grow through our life experiences.

Gardner originally set out to discover what defined 'creativity', and soon came to the realisation that we were limited to some extent in our creative processes due to the emphasis put on the linguistic and logical intelligence tests given to children in schools. He felt that there was more to the story, and first identified other intelligences in his book *Frames of Mind*. These other intelligences included linguistic, logical-mathematical, visual-spatial, musical, bodily-kinaesthetic and personal intelligence (which was later divided).

In Gardner's original research, he set out criteria for the intelligences:
- One important criterion was that the intelligences were located in specific areas of the brain and could be lost or impaired due to trauma.
- Another stated that prodigies in a particular talent existed, and that these intelligences were present throughout human history. In addition, they were found worldwide and were not based on cultural practices but rooted in biology.
- The intelligences also lent themselves to a coding system and symbols which captured the main information demonstrated by the skill. In research experiments, Gardner also claimed that the intelligences could be determined through administering standardised tests.

'I believe that the brain has evolved over millions of years to be responsive to different kinds of content in the world. Language content, musical content, spatial content, numerical content, etc.'
Howard Gardner

Soon after the original theory was published, he separated the *personal* intelligence into 'interpersonal' and 'intrapersonal'. In 1997, he added the *natural* intelligence, and has been looking into the possibility of adding an ethical or moral one.

Their use in the classroom has been explored by a number of writers, and activities geared towards the different intelligences can be found throughout the ELT literature, as well as in books on educational practice. Some of them overlap with the styles chosen in *Spotlight on Learning Styles* – although they may be used in different ways.

The intelligences, however, seem to exercise a great influence on what types of *jobs* we take and what we do in our free time. This may be less apparent in looking at the other styles. An example would be that a musical and kinaesthetic person may become a dancer, figure skater or choreographer, while a visual-spatial and kinaesthetic person may choose a career as a carpenter or sculptor. The VAK or Global–Analytic models, taken by themselves, may be less likely to have as strong an influence on the choice of a career.

Neuro-Linguistic Programming

NLP is increasingly mentioned in various ELT and other educational literature. Although the initial training in NLP begins with the VAK model, it is not a learning style in itself.

In the 1970s, Richard Bandler and John Grinder began studying the connection between linguistics and psychology. They observed three well-known and successful therapists – Virginia Satir (family therapy), Fritz Perls (Gestalt therapy) and Milton Erickson (hypnotherapy).

'Problems are not the problem; coping is the problem.'
Virginia Satir

'Learning is the discovery that something is possible.'
Fritz Perls

'A goal without a date is just a dream.'
Milton Erickson

In order to investigate the use of verbal and non-verbal communication and their effect on success with patients, Bandler and Grinder recorded hours of video which they later analysed. They discovered that these three therapists were able to establish rapport and trust with clients in a way that piqued their interest and led to further studies in the field and a coding of their results. Amongst the first commonalities that Bandler and Grinder noticed

Further approaches

were the language patterns which they later sorted into the VAK model, similar to the one researched by Swassing and Barbe.

As Bandler and Grinder were particularly interested in the psychological ramifications of communication, NLP was first conceived as a short-term therapy. It is based on the concept of establishing successful communication strategies in order to reach specific goals, and can be used as a method of self-discovery and personal development.

- After its initial use in the world of psychology, businesspeople began to realise that NLP could be used to improve communication in the workplace.
- Soon after, it also moved into the sphere of education and counselling. In creating effective communicative situations, knowing how another person perceives information can be used as a foundation leading to better relationships, trust or being better able to convince someone else of your point of view.

All these elements can, of course, be extremely useful in the classroom, but the VAK model also stands alone as a learning style. When NLP is implemented in the classroom today, it is used for things such as classroom management, working with at-risk students, anchoring positive behaviour to help discover successful learning strategies or for helping educators and learners to set realistic goals. (See Grinder, *Righting the Educational Conveyor Belt*.)

NLP has continued to develop through the work of people like Robert Dilts and Judith DeLozier, both of whom have looked at learning in general, and have created practical applications to help people achieve their goals and learn a number of techniques. Techniques such as conflict resolution, establishing new patterns of communication in dealing with others, goal-setting, and creativity strategies – to name only a few.

In the field of ELT, Jane Revell and Susan Norman have published books on using NLP techniques in the English classroom, and have developed a wide variety of language-based activities which can be applied in a number of settings.

Environmental Preferences

Rita and Kenneth Dunn have researched and published widely in the field of learning styles and are well known for their work on 'environmental preferences'. The Dunns felt that there were at least 18 elements, consisting of four basic stimuli, which affect absorption and retention of information.

They created a self-reporting instrument in 1978 called the 'Learning Styles Inventory' (not to be confused with the LSI developed by Kolb), targeted at different age groups to find out how these external factors influenced learning: factors such as temperature, light, sounds, time of day, motivation, group or individual work, etc, which were classified into environmental, emotional, sociological and physical stimuli. The survey is scored by computer and teachers can receive individual scores or a summary for an entire group.

The studies are fascinating and the scores can be extremely helpful for both obtaining a general picture of a group and their needs, as well as for giving tips to learners for learning at home – making it a useful counselling tool, especially for learners who are having difficulties and searching for help to improve their performance. Although some group patterns may emerge, it may not always be possible to implement any necessary changes in the classroom.

It would be difficult to find language activities based on the environmental preferences as such, which is the reason they have not been included in Part B of this book. A one-to-one counselling situation would be the place to give tips to individual students on how to work better on the four skills and on learning vocabulary and grammar, but these styles are much more individual than the ones on which we have chosen to base our activities.

Further activities

Spotlight on Learning Styles is designed for ELT teachers – the activities in Part B have been created to aid language learning, and contain specific linguistic goals and aims. They generally practise a particular aspect of grammar, vocabulary or structure, and can be used as an impetus to encourage conversation in the classroom. In addition, the suggestions for extending the activities may include homework as well as writing practice – to encourage the variety of skills necessary for learning a language.

- The activities can be used with any school or coursebook as supplementary material, or used on their own if the teacher feels the need to concentrate more on a particular aspect of the language.
- They can also be used to provide variety in the classroom and help the learners enjoy language learning.

However, there are *other* activities which can be done, based on our learning style models, to work on communication and self-awareness of the individual styles. If these are also carried out in English, they can be used as part of an English lesson.

Given that the goal of the activities below is not to create language but awareness of styles, these activities can be done either in English or in the mother tongue. This would depend on the level of language proficiency of the learners, as well as the ultimate aim of the teacher in making use of these ideas and suggestions for the classroom.

Reflecting on the activities and discussing reactions to them is an excellent way to help learners not only become aware of their own styles but also understand that others may do things in totally different ways, based on their styles.

Raising awareness of VAK perceptual abilities

Input, output and storage

In this VAK activity, the learners can experiment with their input and output channels to discover the processes they go through to perceive and recall information.

(Note: This activity uses the kinaesthetic motoric channel, but not the emotional one.)

- Using small objects like buttons or coins, the learners work in pairs and lay the objects in front of them with the goal of getting their partner to recreate the same pattern after *looking* at the items (V), *hearing* the partner say them aloud (A) or by *touching* them with their eyes closed (K).

- The recommended way to do this is to use a total of twelve objects for each person, consisting of four identical or very similar objects divided into three different colours, shapes or textures. For example, you can use four one-cent coins, four matchsticks and four buttons of the same size and colour for each person, resulting in a total of three groups of eight similar objects, divided equally between the pair:

Person A:　○ ○ ○ ○　　□ □ □ □　　△ △ △△

Person B:　○ ○ ○ ○　　□ □ □ □　　△ △ △△

- By changing the *input* method, as above, learners become more familiar with their preferred perceptual strengths and begin to realise how they go about receiving information.

- The *output* method can be changed, as well, by asking the learners to lay out the pattern or describe it after having seen, heard or touched the items, giving them the opportunity to reflect on this aspect of learning too.

- This works best when the learners begin with a small number of objects (four or five) and

Further activities

increase the number (up to the twelve available) until the partner can no longer repeat the pattern.

○ At this point, it is useful to find out what strategies the learners use to help them remember – as this gives insight into the strengths of their VAK channels.

In this activity, the learners experiment in pairs to find out which methods of input and output they prefer, and are encouraged to then think about what they need in order to successfully store the information.

It is important to remember that, as teachers, we can influence the *input* (how we present material) and the *output* of information (how we 'test' it) but we cannot influence the *storage* – as that happens within the individual learner's brain and body.

This is based on the idea of the Swassing-Barbe Modality Index, a kit containing objects which can be used to determine modality strength.

'Sensation, perception and memory constitute what we are calling modality.'
Walter Barbe and Raymond Swassing

Note: I learned this activity in a teacher training course with Michael Grinder in Portland, Oregon – the description of how Michael uses it can be found in his book *Righting the Educational Conveyor Belt*.

 My favourite place

Another VAK activity is to put the learners in a group of four and ask one person to sit in the middle.

○ This person names their favourite place. The other three then make one sentence each about the place, using one of the sensory channels. For example, if the person in the middle loves the sea:

- The learner using the visual channel might say:
  'Perhaps you see the blue of the sea and the sun sparkling on the waves.'
- The person using the auditory channel could say:
  'Perhaps you hear the sound of the surf hitting the beach.'
- The person using the kinesthaetic channel could say:
  'Perhaps you feel the sun on your head and the water on your toes.'

○ When all three have finished their sentences, the person in the middle says which of the sentences was their favourite.

This activity can help to determine the type of sensory-based language a person may need to make an experience as real as possible. It also gives the others the chance to practise using different sensory-based language, a skill which takes a certain amount of practice and can be expanded on in language lessons, especially when working on communicative abilities.

(Note: The kinaesthetic emotional channel can be added here as well. The group would then consist of five – and the two people making kinaesthetic statements would be instructed to concentrate on the tactile aspect or the emotional aspect in their sentences.)

 The telephone strategy game

'Sometimes hanging in there is what you need to do, even in the face of frustration.'
Robert Dilts

This VAK activity (developed by Robert Dilts in *Dynamic Learning*) also uses different input and output channels and gives the learners the chance to make use of all of them while practising language and non-verbal communication skills at the same time.

(Note: The activity uses the kinaesthetic motoric channel – but not the emotional one.)

○ Put the learners into groups of four (A, B, C and D):

- Learner C and Learner D close their eyes.
- Learner A stands up and assumes a pose, which Learner B draws.
- Learner A resumes a normal sitting position.
- Learner B gives their drawing to Learner C, who describes it to Learner D.
- Learner D listens to the description and tries to assume the same pose as Learner A.

○ Once Learner D has completed the pose, Learner A assumes the original pose and the group compares them.

○ The activity continues until each person has taken on each of the roles.

This lively game is an excellent way to help learners think about their VAK strengths, and how they use them in new situations.

○ The activity can also be changed by getting Learner B to explain the pose to C and letting C draw it. Learner D would then assume the pose, based on the drawing rather than listening to the description.

○ Another alternative is to ask Learner B to write out what A is doing in the pose rather than drawing it, and Learner C reads the description and makes a drawing which they give to D to act out.

There are a number of ways to adapt this activity, but the important part is asking the learners to think about their own reactions to it:
Which part was easiest or most difficult?
How can they relate this information to their own learning strategies and situations?
Did they discover anything about themselves which they can use to develop into successful learners or apply to specific situations in which they need to learn something new?

Raising awareness of Global–Analytic learner types

The characteristics sorting game

Increasing awareness of the way global and analytic learners process information can give them valuable insights into how their minds work.

An activity where the learners have to talk about their specific experiences can be done with cards.

○ Copy and cut out the cards on page 112.

○ Distribute the cards to the learners and ask them to choose the ones they think suit them best.

○ Now tell each of them to choose one card with a characteristic which they feel is one of the most important to them. They then think of an example in their own experience which best describes this particular characteristic and tell the class about it. For example: *'I really enjoyed the last lesson when I worked in a group because I like all the people and we have fun together.'*

○ The class then guess which characteristic the person is describing (eg relationship-oriented).

○ The next step is to place the cards in two areas of the room:

- In one area, they put the cards they feel are more *global*.
- In the other, those they feel are more *analytic*.

○ They can then see if the cards they chose for themselves fall more into one category than the other.

'This exercise is a basic metaphor for a strategy and can help you build intuitions about what makes a good strategy. If the group of people represented a brain, the sequence of transformations might be a learning strategy. Each person in the group is like a step in somebody's strategy for learning something.'
Robert Dilts

'Field-dependence-independence appears to be more related to the 'how' than the 'how much' of cognitive function.'
Herman Witkin

Further activities

If this activity is carried out before doing the Checklist questionnaire on page 32, the questionnaire results can subsequently be compared with the activity and discussed.

A further point would be to ask the learners to reflect on the learning situations in which they use one ability rather than another. Ask them to look for patterns to determine what they usually do. They should think about the characteristics and if they are dependent on the task in hand, or if they are a general approach.

Global	Analytic
○ needs the 'big picture'	○ focuses on the details
○ enjoys groupwork	○ likes to work alone
○ is intuitive, perceptive and imaginative	○ is rational and logical
○ makes associations between different pieces of information	○ likes to work step-by-step
○ waits to see what will happen	○ needs to know what to expect
○ works to please others	○ is self-motivated
○ works on several projects at a time	○ finishes one thing at a time
○ likes to be personally involved with others in the group	○ does not become personally involved with others in the group
○ is more affected by criticism	○ is less affected by criticism
○ avoids competition	○ likes competition
○ values feelings over facts	○ values facts over feelings
○ is relationship-oriented	○ is task-oriented
○ is options-oriented	○ is procedures-oriented
○ lives for the moment	○ likes to plan ahead
○ remembers the whole experience	○ remembers individual facts

Further activities

Raising awareness of Mind Organisation styles

 Working with your own style

A good follow-up activity for the Mind Organisation Index questionnaire on page 34 is to separate the class into groups according to their *preferred* style.

○ Give the groups paper and a task where they talk about certain aspects of their personalities, and discuss how they go about learning something new. They can prepare a class excursion and write out the plan and the steps. Or they can make posters which reflect certain aspects of their personalities – what their work space looks like, what their hobbies are, or where their favourite place is and why, etc.

○ When they have finished, compare the different posters and look at the main differences between them.

○ Ask the groups to discuss among themselves how they went about making decisions while working on their ideas and how they planned their posters.

○ Tell the groups that it is helpful if they share their knowledge – if they tell the class how they went about solving a problem and the methods they used. You can make notes on the board and, at the end, compare them to see if there were any striking similarities or differences. When these stand out, you can go back to the diagram on page 22 to see if similarities occurred more in groups which shared *perceptual* or *organisational* preferences.

○ There is no right or wrong to this activity – it is simply a way of giving insight and demonstrating that different roads can lead to the same place: a concept which enables teamwork and may be vital to the final result.

Working with mixed styles

A second activity, when working with style groups, is to form groups consisting of learners of *different* styles:

○ Give the groups a task to do (such as solving a puzzle or planning a project for the future) and a time limit. When they have finished, ask them to analyse how they went about this.

○ Find out if the *mixed* group worked differently from a group of the *same* style.

○ Ask them to analyse the work and the processes which ocurred in the groups, and to think about the different roles that the group members played. They can then look back at the characteristics given in the Mind Organisation section and compare how the people in the group acted with the descriptions of the four learner types.

○ A reflection period can be added: to get the learners to think back about the work they did together, and whether they felt more comfortable with some people than with others. They should be encouraged to try and figure out what made it comfortable or less comfortable.

○ The last task that either the group or the individuals can do is to speculate on the outcome and think about whether it would have been different if groups of the *same* style had worked together rather than *mixing* the styles.

○ Individual learners can also be asked if another group member made a suggestion that they feel they themselves would not have thought of at all – and if they found this helpful.

This type of activity can be used for team building – and to make it clear why people of different styles are often necessary on a team in order to achieve a result which can be put into practice.

'At the most basic level, students became aware that they are unique individuals and perceive the world in different ways.'
April Bowie

'Awareness is only the first step in the process of encouraging successful learners; utilising the strategies is the key to developing life-long learning habits.'
April Bowie

'Being able to identify personal characteristics and acknowledge those same attributes in others creates in one a sense of acceptance and appreciation.'
April Bowie

Further reading

Once you have begun to delve into the world of learning styles, you may find that you have become interested in gaining more knowledge and information about such a fascinating field. There are many approaches to this, as demonstrated in the styles we concentrated on earlier in *Spotlight on Learning Styles* and in the further ideas mentioned in Part C.

A list of publications is provided here to accompany you on this journey.

Some of these were already mentioned in their contexts, and others will take you down a different path altogether.

As this is a path best discovered by the individual, the list is an invitation to continue to take in new ideas, concepts and possibilities – within your own learning environment – and hopefully will encourage you to continue doing what you enjoy, as well as to take on new challenges and experiment with further ideas, as both teacher and life-long learner.

Learning styles

Barbe, W B and Swassing, R H *Teaching Through Modality Strengths: Concepts and Practices* Zaner-Bloser Inc. 1979

Barrett, S L *It's All in Your Head* Free Spirit Publishing 1985

Bowie, A *Adolescent Self Perceptions of Learning Styles: A Qualitative Study* Master's Thesis, Antioch University, Seattle 1998

Butler, K *Learning and Teaching Style in Theory and Practice* The Learner's Dimension 1987

Dunn, R and Dunn, K *Teaching Students Through Their Individual Learning Styles* Prentice Hall 1978

Dunn, R and Dunn, K *The Complete Guide to the Learning Styles Inservice System* Allyn and Bacon 1999

Gregorc, A *An Adult's Guide to Style* Gregorc Associates 1982

Guild, P B and Garger, S *Marching to Different Drummers* Association for Supervision and Curriculum Development (ASCD) 1998

Keefe, J W 'Learning styles: an overview' in Keefe, J W (Ed): *Student learning styles: Diagnosing and prescribing programs* Reston, VA: National Association of Secondary School Principals 1979

Kline, P *The Everyday Genius: Restoring Children's Natural Joy of Learning – And Yours Too* Great Open Publishers 1988

Kolb, D *Experiential Learning: Experience as the Source of Learning and Development* Prentice Hall 1984

König, M E *Theory of Learning Styles and Practical Applications* Grin-Verlag für akademische Texte 2005

Markova, D *How Your Child Is Smart* Conari Press 1992

McCarthy, B *The 4MAT® System* Excel Inc. 1987

Pritchard, A *Ways of Learning: Learning Theories and Learning Styles in the Classroom* David Fulton Publishers 2005

Rainey, M A and Kolb, D 'Using Experiential Learning Theory and Learning Styles in Diversity Education' in *The Importance of Learning Styles* Sims, R R and Sims, S J (Eds) Greenwood Press 1995

Reid, J *Learning Styles in the ESL/EFL Classroom* Heinle and Heinle 1995

Renner, P *The Art of Teaching Adults* PFR Training Associates Ltd. 1994

Roche, T *Investigating Learning Style in the Foreign Language Classroom* Langenscheidt 2006

Rosenberg, M 'Learning and Styles: Learner-Differentiated Approaches and Methods' in *Looking at Learning* Waxman 2011

Further reading

Sims, R R and Sims, S J (Eds) *The Importance of Learning Styles* Greenwood Press 1995

Williams, L V *Teaching for the Two-Sided Mind* Simon & Schuster Inc. 1983

Witkin, H A 'A cognitive approach to cross-cultural research' *International Journal of Psychology* 2 (4) 1967

Witkin, H A and Goodenough, D R *Cognitive Styles: Essence and Origins* International Universities Press 1981

http://www.touchmath.com/pdf/Seminar_Swassing.pdf

http://peo.cambridge.org/index.php?option=com_content&view=article&id=1:a-learning-styles- approach-to-activities-for-the-business-english-classroom-by-marjorie-rosenberg&catid=2:general-articles&Itemid=8

http://chiasuanchong.com/2012/05/13/devils-advocate-vs-marjorie-rosenberg-on-learning-styles/

http://www.developingteachers.com/articles_tchtraining/tdev1_marjorie.htm

Multiple Intelligences

Armstrong, T *In Their Own Way* Jeremy P Tarcher/Putnam 1987

Berman, M *A Multiple Intelligences Road to an ELT Classroom* Crowne House Publishing 1998

Gardner, H *Frames of Mind* Basic Books 1983

Gardner, H *To Open Minds* Basic Books 1989

Gardner, H *Multiple Intelligences* Basic Books 1993

http://hmt.myweb.uga.edu/webwrite/gardner.htm

http://howardgardner.com/multiple-intelligences/

NLP

Bandler, R and Grinder, J *Frogs into Princes* Real People Press 1979

Beaver, D *Lazy Learning* Element 1996

Dilts, R *Dynamic Learning* Meta Publications 1995

Grinder, M *Righting the Educational Conveyor Belt* Metamorphous Press 1991

Grinder, M *ENVoY: Your personal guide to classroom management* Michael Grinder & Associates 1993

Hager, M *Target Fluency: Leading Edge Foreign Language Teaching Techniques* Metamorphous Press 1994

Lloyd, L *Classroom Magic* Metamorphous Press 1990

Mahony, T *Words Work! How to change your language to improve behavior in your classroom* Crown House Publishing 2003

O'Connor, J and Seymour, J *Introducing Neuro-Linguistic Programming* Mandala 1990

Revell, J and Norman, S *In Your Hands: NLP in ELT* Saffire Press 1997

Revell, J and Norman, S *Handing Over: NLP-based activities for language learning* Saffire Press 1999

Rosenberg, M 'The How of Thinking: The Secrets of Neuro-Linguistic Programming' *Analytic Teaching, The Community of Enquiry Journal* 20 (2) Viterbo University 2000

Van Nagel, C, Reese, E J, Reese, M and Siudzinski, R *Mega Teaching and Learning* Metamorphous Press 1985

http://www.nlpu.com/NewDesign/NLPU_WhatIsNLP.html

http://www.viterbo.edu/analytic/vol%2020%20no.%202/the%20how%20of%20thinking.pdf

Classroom strategies and activities

Benson, P *Autonomy in Language Learning* Pearson 2001

Dörnyei, Z *Motivational Strategies in the Language Classroom* CUP 2001

Hadfield, J *Classroom Dynamics* Oxford University Press 1992

Harmer, J *The Practice of English Language Teaching* Longman 2007

Jug, B and Weitlaner, U *mehr als bloß spielen* Eigenverlag 2007

Puchta, H and Williams, M *Teaching Young Learners to Think* Helbling Languages 2012

Scharle, A and Szabó, A *Learner Autonomy* CUP 2000

Schmitt, N (Ed) *An Introduction to Applied Linguistics* Hodder Education 2002

Wingate, J *Knowing Me, Knowing You* Delta Publishing 2000

Woodward, T *Planning Lessons and Courses* CUP 2001

http://www.developingteachers.com/articles_tchtraining/articles_index3.htm

https://netfiles.umn.edu/users/adcohen/2010%20-%20Styles%2C%20Strategies%2C%20and%20Motivation%20in%20Schmitt.pdf?uniq=-jhw8zt

From spotlight to springboard

The activities we have included in *Spotlight on Learning Styles* are meant to be flexible and provide ideas for further development – with slight changes to suit levels, class sizes or different learning styles.

The idea of this book is to serve as a springboard to creativity and fun in the classroom, while allowing both the teacher and the learner to discover the joy in the act of learning:

- When we choose activities to suit a group, they run by themselves – the problems arise when we try to fit a square peg into a round hole.
- When we understand how we can adapt activities to make them suitable for a group of learners, our chances of creating an optimal learning environment increase.

The aim in writing a book like this is to share ideas which have worked in a variety of settings with a large variety of learners – in order to help other teachers on the road to discovery.

Self-awareness which comes out of lessons on learning styles can be the first step. But going on to make the most of an individual's style is an invaluable tool which will serve both the learner and teacher for years to come.

As a teacher, teacher trainer and communicator, I cannot imagine a greater gift to give to anyone.

Enjoy using *Spotlight on Learning Styles* – and remember that life-long learning is one of the most natural, as well as basic, characteristics that humans all share.

From the editors

Spotlight on Learning Styles focuses on *how* we learn – rather than *what* we learn. Based on her academic research and her practical experience as both teacher and teacher trainer, Marjorie Rosenberg has written an authoritative but accessible resource book on learner styles, effectively spotlighting our individual learning preferences and what we can all do to teach – and to learn – more successfully.

She demonstrates, most convincingly, that if teachers recognise the characteristics of their own teaching and learning styles, and if learners recognise the characteristics of their own learning styles, we can work together to multiply the possibilities for success.

Spotlight on Learning Styles contains three distinctive parts which focus in turn on theory, practice and development:

Part A explains the importance of learning styles, concentrating on three differentiated models – rooted in sensory perception, cognitive processing and behavioural studies – where teachers discover how they are teaching and understand how their learners are learning.

Part B provides a wealth of activities – in the form of strategies which focus on the learning style models one by one, and which involve and motivate all the learners – and demonstrates how an awareness of learning styles can lead to a more inclusive and successful classroom.

Part C focuses on further development – further approaches to learning styles, further activities that go beyond the purely linguistic, and further reading for those who wish to know more – and reminds us that teaching is a profession that involves life-long learning.

Spotlight on Learning Styles provides a springboard for successful learning, successful teaching and successful ongoing development.

Mike Burghall
Lindsay Clandfield

From the publisher

DELTA TEACHER DEVELOPMENT SERIES

A pioneering award-winning series of books for English Language Teachers
with professional development in mind.

Spotlight on Learning Styles
by Marjorie Rosenberg
ISBN 978-1-905085-71-2

The Book of Pronunciation
by Jonathan Marks and
Tim Bowen
ISBN 978-1-905085-70-5

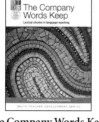

The Company Words Keep
by Paul Davis and
Hanna Kryszewska
ISBN 978-1-905085-20-0

Digital Play
by Kyle Mawer and
Graham Stanley
ISBN 978-1-905085-55-2

Teaching Online
by Nicky Hockly with
Lindsay Clandfield
ISBN 978-1-905085-35-4

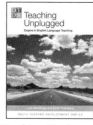

Teaching Unplugged
by Luke Meddings and
Scott Thornbury
ISBN 978-1-905085-19-4

Culture in our Classrooms
by Gill Johnson and
Mario Rinvolucri
ISBN 978-1-905085-21-7

The Developing Teacher
by Duncan Foord
ISBN 978-1-905085-22-4

Being Creative
by Chaz Pugliese
ISBN 978-1-905085-33-0

The Business English Teacher
by Debbie Barton,
Jennifer Burkart and
Caireen Sever
ISBN 978-1-905085-34-7

For details of these and future titles in the series,
please contact the publisher: *E-mail* info@deltapublishing.co.uk
Or visit the DTDS website at www.deltapublishing.co.uk/titles/methodology